Anonymous

The City and County of El Paso, Texas

Containing useful and reliable information concerning the future great

metropolis of the Southwest: its resources and advantages for the

agriculturist, artisan and capitalist

Anonymous

The City and County of El Paso, Texas
Containing useful and reliable information concerning the future great metropolis of the Southwest: its resources and advantages for the agriculturist, artisan and capitalist

ISBN/EAN: 9783337236731

Printed in Europe, USA, Canada, Australia, Japan

Cover: Foto ©Lupo / pixelio.de

More available books at **www.hansebooks.com**

THE CITY AND COUNTY

OF

EL PASO, TEXAS,

CONTAINING USEFUL AND RELIABLE INFORMATION CONCERNING

THE FUTURE GREAT METROPOLIS OF THE SOUTHWEST

ITS RESOURCES AND ADVANTAGES

FOR THE

AGRICULTURIST, ARTISAN AND CAPITALIST.

———————•———————

1886.

TIMES PUBLISHING CO.,

EL PASO, TEXAS.

PREFACE.

The little work which we here offer has been prepared in more of a hurry than we could obviate, as our time and business engagements while occupied upon it did not permit of that application to it of attention and labor which a due performance of the undertaking really demanded. Nevertheless, we send it forth as it is, with the assurance that we have set forth with equal fidelity the advantages and disadvantages of our county and locality; and we stand ready to verify them.

No organized effort of the kind has heretofore been attempted; this fact, among others, suggested to us the advantages we might reasonably expect from such organized and well directed effort, furnishing reliable and authentic information, by an authoritative source. But far above any other motive, we are actuated by a desire to labor in the task of elevating El Paso County, and the large area of country that must be dependent upon and tributary to it (which therefore must enrich it), to that high position in the world of wealth and business to which her natural resources and her natural advantages certainly give her a commanding claim.

The population of El Paso County hitherto has not, unfortunately, been of the progressive kind. The Spanish or Mexican Indian races of whom, until the advent of the railways, four years ago, about ninety-nine hundredths of the population was composed, and of which one-half of it is still composed—has caused the country to progress scarcely a move in the great march of material wealth and improvement, beyond what it was in the days of the Spanish vice-royalty in Mexico, to which it was once subject. Up to that time (1881) this was practically a " terra incognita."

(3)

Surely it is time now that one of the oldest, most attractive, and best counties in the great State of Texas, and yet the least known until the epoch of the railroads, should enter the lists for the championship of them all.

Like the sleeping giant, El Paso County and the great country she represents (for reasons which we will hereafter demonstrate), has been reposing in the consciousness of her strength and power, to arise when the time should come, by the very force of her inherent strength, and to assume among the great natural and political divisions of her own State, and of the busy world, the position and rank to which the laws of Nature and Nature's God entitle her.

El Paso, Texas.

INTRODUCTORY.

This pamphlet is issued by the EL PASO BUREAU OF INFORMATION, an organization composed of many of the principal citizens of El Paso County, Texas. Its objects and purposes are: To diffuse and impart, by publication, correspondence, and otherwise as may seem best, useful, clear and reliable information concerning our county, its resources, attractions, advantages and capabilities, with a view to encourage and promote immigration; to assist in finding homes for the immigrant; to attract capital by the suggestion of advantages; to induce its investment; and to do all things within its power and purpose to secure and achieve the objects for which it was organized. We trust, therefore, that all persons into whose hands this pamphlet may fall will peruse carefully its contents, and then place it in the hands of others, to whom it may not only be of interest, but prove a blessing; and at the same time forward to the Bureau here the names of acquaintances who would be likely to be interested in it.

The following named persons compose the "Central Committee" of the organization:

OFFICERS.

President,,	Hon. T. A. FALVEY,	District Judge.
1st Vice-President,	S. H. BUCHANAN,	Builder.
2d Vice-President,	S. W. BORING,	City Marshal.
Treasurer,	FIRST NAT. BANK,	El Paso.

MEMBERS.

J. F. SATTERTHWAITE,	Capitalist.
J. P. HAGUE,	Attorney-at-Law.
JAMES MARR,	El Paso Transfer Co.
W. M. DAVIS,	Hardware Merchant.
H. M. MUNDY,	Dealer in Land and Live Stock.
JOSEPH SCHUTZ,	Wholesale Dry Goods.
C. E. MOORMAN,	Attorney-at-Law.
F. C. GAY,	Agent A., T. & S. F. R'y.
J. C. BEATTY,	Mgr. Mex. & Tex. Land & Cattle Co.
R. C. LIGHTBODY,	Clothing & Furnishing Goods.
W. B. McLACHLIN,	Real Estate & Insurance.
A. KRAKAUER,	Gen'l Merchant.
R. F. CAMPBELL,	Druggist.
E. C. ROBERTS,	Merchant.
JOHN JULIAN,	Merchant.
J. A. McKINNEY,	Physician.
H. S. KAUFMAN,	Cashier First Nat Bank.
H. W. READ,	Baptist Minister and Evangelist.
C. R. MOREHEAD,	Pres't State Nat. Bank.
HENRY BENEKE,	Hardware Merchant.
WM. WATTS,	El Paso Water Works.
BENJ. SCHUSTER,	Gen'l Merchant.
CHAS. MERRICK,	Clothing & Furnishing.
W. A. IRVIN,	Drugs & Chemicals.
Dr. ROSSER,	Physician.
JOSEPH GIST,	Real Estate Dealer.
CHAS. T. RACE,	Physician.
E. V. BERRIEN,	Furniture.
J. R. CURRIE,	Capitalist.
J. G. BROCK,	Real Estate & Live Stock.
JOSEPH MAGOFFIN,	Collector of Customs.
H. L. DETWILER,	Contractor.
F. N. HOLBROOK,	Mining Engineer.
J. H. BATE,	"Daily Times."

SIGNIFICANCE OF THE NAME "EL PASO."

Two Spanish words, meaning "The Pass." It will be necessary for the reader to bear this in mind, as he will see, not only by reading this book, but by a glance at any map, old or new, how appropriately the name has been applied. How unerringly has the finger of destiny pointed toward this place—this "Pass" through the mountains—this great natural highway from North to South, from East to West—this great geographical and commercial center!

CITY OF EL PASO.

This city is no doubt destined to become the great commercial and political metropolis of this vast region. Nature has given her the position, and the laws of trade, like those of nature, will always assert themselves. Our position relatively, and very significantly, is about equidistant from the great cities of Mexico, San Francisco, St. Louis, New Orleans, Kansas City, and Galveston—about eleven hundred miles from each; too far to come into competition or rivalry with any of them, and having direct and competitive railroad communication with all of them. And all of them are now competing for our trade, and for the trade of Mexico through us. This is in many respects, perhaps, the most important and brilliant commercial prospect we have; and the rich traffic that it promises, and results that must follow, cannot be over estimated. The commerce of Chihuahua, Durango, Zacatecas, and other Mexican States, which are cut off from the ocean by high mountain barriers, is now passing through this city in a steady stream. One commission house here paid duties, within the last year, on goods and merchandise consigned to Mexico, of $367,000, and this represents about one-sixth of the total amount of duties paid at this point on goods destined for Mexico during the same period. The vast extent of territory tributary to this city, and her exact position in the pathway of the immense trade that will, in the course of time, be carried on between the two Republics and with the States of Central and South America, by means of railroad systems now in operation or projected, and with the West India Islands, China, and Japan, by means of her railroads to the Pacific, give her commercial future a magnitude the mind can scarcely grasp. In point of destiny, we believe that El Paso is entitled to rank with any of the great cities we have named, and that, before she is as old as Kansas City or Denver now are, she will have outstripped either of them. This is no visionary view. We are better entitled to say this now, we have more in sight, more ground for our belief, than the wildest enthusiast could have claimed for either of those cities ten years ago. With improved means of intercourse, and better commercial treaties with these States and countries just mentioned, a commerce of enormous value will be maintained with the United States, much of which must pass through here. A fact that will seem incredible to many, as it has no doubt escaped general observation, is, that the Mexican Central Railway, in its 1,225 miles between here and the City of Mexico, passes through twenty-one cities (including the two termini) having a population of 950,000. And, as we have already shown, we are in the centre of a great district, including Western Texas, Southern New Mexico, and Eastern Arizona, the trade of which we shall undoubtedly command; the importance of which is, of itself, sufficient to build up a great city.

In addition to the five railroads already terminating here, we have the prospect of others. The first is that to the White Oaks coal fields. This road will not only **bring us** cheap coal in abundance (when reduction **works,** glass works, and many other manufacturing en- **terprises** will soon follow), but it will bring the ores **from the** many mines discovered near its route, and the **lumber and** timber from the great White Mountain dis- **trict; it will** also be extended so as to connect with the **St.** Louis & San Francisco Railroad, which, when com- pleted, will give a line from El Paso to St. Louis two **hundred and** fifty miles shorter than by any other route.

We can confidently ask, Is there, or has there been, **such a prospect in** view for any town in the United States?

Thus much for our prospects; now as to the city **itself.**

A little more than four years ago there were less than **200 persons** here, all told; no railroads, no modern im- **provements,** nothing but a few old adobe structures; and **the town was** almost unworthy of a name. To-day we **have five railroads—the** prospect just spoken of for the **completion of** others—and we have a population of at **least 5,500 as** wideawake and intelligent people as can **anywhere be** found. The old adobe buildings are fast giving way **to** business blocks as substantial and elegant **as can be found in** Texas; while of residence property **there has** been erected, on all sides of the business center, properties which have transformed an open com- **mon into a** beautiful city of comfortable and elegant **homes.** Of churches there are substantial structures **owned by** the Episcopal, Methodist, Baptist, Presbyte- **rian, and** Catholic societies. We have two well-equipped **planing mills,** three brickyards which carry from one **and a half to two and** a half millions of brick in stock, **of good quality, and in** color from a deep red to a Milwaukee straw color. Our lumber yards are supplied from Eastern Texas, Arkansas, Louisiana, New Mexico, California, and Nevada. Lumber is worth from $25 to $40 per M, according to class. Brick are worth $10 per M, laid in the wall. It is estimated that more than 400 permanent structures have been erected within the past two years, and the builders and contractors were never more active than now; in fact, there is not an idle carpenter or bricklayer in town, and more are needed. Business of all kinds is and has been uniformly good. The depression felt elsewhere so sharply has not affected this place to any noticeable extent; and we claim, confidently, that there is a combination of causes, which can be discovered by the reader from a careful perusal of this pamphlet, that will always operate in favor of this place, and prevent any serious business depression, or any corresponding to that which it is possible to feel elsewhere.

We have an excellent system of water works, with a pressure of 200 pounds, giving us not only plenty of good water for all domestic and manufacturing purposes, but enabling us to have the best protection against fire; and this has induced the organization of a very full and efficient "Fire Department," which is now one of the institutions of the city and a credit to it. We also have gas works, and gas of an excellent quality sold at $2.20 per thousand feet; also electric light works, of the most approved pattern, furnishing an excellent light; the telegraph, of course, and the telephone; two first-class National Banks; two miles and a half of first-class street railway; sampling works, ice factory; opera house, theatre, custom house; one daily and three weekly newspapers; two very fine hotels of the first class, one of which cost $100,000, and several others of the second class; a court house that cost $110,000, and jail costing $35,000; a Live Stock Association, Union Stock

Yards, and a Building Association which has erected 50 houses, costing from $1,000 to $3,500 each; a Transfer Company using 75 animals, and splendidly equipped in every particular (this company alone paid freights on goods and merchandise hauled by them last year of $275,000), and a second of nearly equal capacity. This represents nearly every element of progress.

The city is very eligibly and handsomely situated, on the left bank of the Rio Grande, and the site is everything that could be desired for a great city, combining the needs and beauties of such a situation in a high degree, as to elevation, drainage, scenery, fine sites for residence and business, and general beauty, and, in fact, grandeur of its scenery and surroundings, which far surpass anything of the kind we have ever seen in the Eastern States. One must come West to behold such scenery and such locations for cities, and there they can only be found near or in the Rocky Mountains. There are some drives here—one in particular, just back of the city, that can scarcely be excelled (on account of its great elevation, for the view and fine air that it affords,) by any other drive on the continent so near to a city. Only a mile away is Fort Bliss, the military post to which allusion has already been made, affording another delightful drive over the hills and up the river. But the most interesting drive of all to the stranger is across the river, through the old Mexican town of Paso del Norte, which was founded by the Jesuits in 1620. Everything there will be found of interest to the stranger— the houses, the streets, the people, the old church (built more than 250 years ago), the system of irrigation. The habits, customs, and life of this primitive people are indescribable, as a whole, but very interesting; and their country is beautiful, rich, and susceptible of the highest degree of improvement and cultivation. These people are our neighbors and friends, and our intercourse with them is both pleasant and profitable.

Our city is free from debt, having on hand $3,000; rate of taxation is 25 cents on $100 for general purposes, and 50 cents for school purposes. Under the present charter, the city cannot incur a debt of more than $20,000. The total amount of taxes, State, county, and city, is about $1.75 to the $100.

There are good openings here now for a dairy, a wine manufactory, a **fruit-canning** and beef-canning establishment, a **poultry farm**, a glass factory, smelting and reduction works, a **soap** and candle factory, an apiary, a distillery and brewery, cracker factory, foundry and machine shop, and many other enterprises too numerous to mention; and above all, there are openings here for 10,000 families of industrious people, and millions of capital can find profitable employment.

TEXAS — HISTORICAL SKETCH.

Texas government underwent many and rapid changes before its territory became a part of this stable country. Up to the year 1821, Texas was a part of Mexico, under the dominion of Spanish viceroys. In that year Mexico renounced her allegiance to Spain, and established a regency. After one year's trial the regency was changed to an imperial government. Then the emperor was deposed and, in 1823, a republican form of government was instituted. This only lasted one year, when it was changed for a federal system, modeled after that of the United States. This lasted ten years, and in 1833 Santa Anna established a military despotism. After three years of turbulence and bloodshed, in which the Texans fought under the Federal flag of Mexico, Texas declared her independence, and in 1836 became an independent Republic, and in 1845 was voluntarily annexed to the United States. Her population at that time could not have exceeded 150,000. By the treaty of annexation Texas retained all her public domain. She sold that which now constitutes a part of New Mexico to the United States, for $10,000,000. With this she paid her debt of $5,000,000, constructed her capital, deaf and dumb, blind, and lunatic asylums, and endowed her public schools with the remainder. The history of Texas since then has been one of grand achievement in all things, and in all respects worthy of her heroic struggle for life, and of her eventful birth. Heretofore, the part which El Paso County has performed in all these grand achievements has of necessity been a very humble one. Up to 1881, her position was so remote and isolated that she could scarcely be said to be a spectator, for she did not see, or scarcely know, what was going on in the great world around her. But now all this is changed, as we will proceed to show; and Texas will hereafter be known as much by our achievements as by her own.

EL PASO COUNTY — HISTORICAL SKETCH.

COVERING AN EPOCH FROM 1827 TO 1880, WITH PRINCIPAL TOPOGRAPHICAL FEATURES, ETC.

The County of El Paso, Texas, is situated in the extreme western part of the State, bounded on the north by New Mexico, on the west by the State of Chihuahua, Mexico, the Rio Grande ("great river") constituting the boundary. It lies between longitude 270° and 290° west from Greenwich, and between latitude 31° and 32° north, the latitude being the same as that of Savannah, Ga., and San Diego, Cal. It has a frontage on the Rio Grande of 147 miles, with a superficial area of 7,000 square miles, or 4,480,000 acres—twice as large as Delaware, as large as Connecticut, and six times as large as Rhode Island. Its surface is diversified with mountains, valleys, and plains, sufficient of each to give variety to the grasses, soil and climate, and picturesqueness to the scenery.

That portion lying along the river, and constituting the valley proper, is an alluvial deposit of as rich and productive soil as can anywhere be found. It varies in width from one to six miles, and, while in many places there are quite heavy growths of timber, there is everywhere sufficient for all purposes of the farm and home. The valley is said to have been settled by the Jesuits in 1620, since which time portions of it have been under successful cultivation. The climate is dry, healthy, and delightful, the rainfall averaging from 12 to 18 inches. and the thermometer rarely indicating above 100°: while the winters are mild, the mercury rarely falling below +20°, the ground is never frozen, and the snowfall, under all circumstances extremely light, never lingers upon the warm, unfrozen earth.

The county now contains a population of about 12.000. distributed as follows: The city of El Paso, the county seat, 5,500; Ysleta, formerly the county seat, 2.000; Socorro, about 1,200; San Elzario, 2,000; Fort Bliss, 300; Concordia, 300; Camp Rice, 200; balance of the county. about 500. All of the above named places, with the exception of El Paso, were colonized upon Spanish grants ceded to the inhabitants in the seventeenth century: the Ysleta (or little island) colony having a grant of

9,000 acres, the Socorro colony of 12,000 acres, and the
San Elzario colony of about 40,000 acres.

In 1827, Don Juan Maria Ponce de Leon, an inhabitant
of Paso del Norte (the Mexican town just across the
river), made an application to his government for a grant
of the land on which El Paso, Texas, is now situated
(this was then Mexican territory). The application of
Leon was granted, and thus was the first settlement of
El Paso begun. Farms, vineyards, and orchards were
soon established, and but little of note occurred to dis-
turb the tranquillity of the peaceful inhabitants of this
delightful valley, except the occasional raids of Indians
for the purpose of robbery, until the war with Mexico
was declared by the United States, when this place was
at once found to possess great military and strategic
importance, on account of its remarkable geographical
location and the physical peculiarities of the surface of
the surrounding country; showing thus early what it has
since proven in so many ways, a veritable gateway into
Mexico. Brig.-Gen. Sterling Price, in his memorable
march across the plains with his regiment in 1847, ac-
companied by the "Missouri Horse," under Col. Ralls,
entered Mexico at this point; so did also the command
of Col. Doniphan. During our civil war, it was alter-
nately occupied by large commands of Confederate and
Federal troops, and was made a depot of supply and
base of operations by the Confederates against New
Mexico and Arizona, while it was again held by the Fed-
erals as a key to the control of those territories. During
much of this period it was occupied as a home station
and terminus of the eastern and western divisions of
the great overland mail and stage system then in opera-
tion; thus again early showing that its geographical
position was commanding and important.

These facts did not escape the keen observation of
many of the old soldiers who had been located, or who

had passed through here during those periods, and many
of them returned to avail themselves of the advantages
of trade, soil, climate, and the general easy and pleasant
conditions under which life and comfort may be maintained here.

The military, strategic, and geographical importance
of this point was also soon recognized by our government, and as early as 1858 a permanent and important
military post was established, and has ever since been
maintained here. During all this period, too, the great
natural advantages of this place, geographically and
commercially, were further strongly indicated by the
passage of the great trade routes from the north into
Mexico, and from the east to Arizona, New Mexico, and
California; the mule, ox trains, and stage coach of those
days moving, of necessity, on the same lines of communication, and governed by the same natural law of trade,
as are now the railroads and telegraph. This feature
was also yet further illustrated in the growth and development of the town and magnificent valley of Paso
del Norte, just across the river from us, where it is said
there was at one time a population of 20,000. It was
from this growth and development that the possibilities
and richness of the valley, the fertility and adaptability
of its soil and climate to the production of almost every
cereal, fruit, and vegetable that is necessary to the comfort and gratification of man or beast, and the salubrity
and healthfulness of the climate, were first practically
revealed to Americans.

During the greater part of the period covered by this
sketch, from 1827 to 1880, constituting the first great
epoch in the history of this county, the population numbered about 5,000, nine-tenths of whom were Mexicans,
and they or their descendants are still here in about the
same number. They had organized a county, were supplied with such schools and churches as satisfied their

aspirations (these were wholly under the control of the Jesuit missions), and were in all respects a law-abiding, happy, and contented people; all, of course, citizens of the United States, having acquired that dignity when Texas achieved her independence from Mexico, after her heroic struggle with that power terminating with the glorious victory of San Jacinto, and became a State of the Union.

In 1878 several great trunk and trans-continental lines of railroad were already projected from and upon points and along lines of latitude and longitude that must of necessity carry them to or through this point and pass. They now vigorously resumed construction. Though none of them were within 600 miles of here, this active resumption of work attracted the attention of a few sagacious Americans who came here during the next two years, to perhaps the number of fifty, to await events still apparently remote. At that time (1878) there were but 23 Americans in what is now the city of El Paso, and about 150 Mexicans. A small garrison of soldiers was quartered in the town, which consisted of a number of old adobe houses of the pure Mexican type. So nondescript, unique, and picturesque were these structures, to the unaccustomed eye, that any effort to describe them would, we fear, fail to convey a correct impression. The metropolis of the county was then at Ysleta, thirteen miles below El Paso, on the river, where the District Court was held and the county business was transacted, and where there was a Mexican population of about 2,000. During the years 1879 and 1880, the great railroads approaching here—the Atchison, Topeka & Santa Fé from the north, the Southern Pacific from the west, the Texas & Pacific and the Galveston, Harrisburg & San Antonio from the east—pushed their work of construction so vigorously, that increased attention was directed to this place; and before the end of the year 1880,

2

though the railroads were still more than 100 miles distant, the first sound and wave of the coming "boom" had struck El Paso, and aroused the sleepy old adobe town from its fifty years of lethargy. The soldiers were obliged to give up their quarters to the citizens. The town was evacuated, in the military sense, and turned over to the mob of enterprising, active spirits who were crowding in from every direction. All sorts of new enterprises, suitable to the demands and prospects, were inaugurated; building began, town lots advanced; railroad officials, surveying parties, contractors and their employés began to make their appearance upon our streets, inspiring renewed hope and confidence in our future. Then, about the beginning of 1881, began the most marvelous display of energy in railroad construction that has perhaps ever been witnessed—the grand struggle of four important trans-continental lines to secure advantages of location and business by first reaching this place. All of these roads have direct or continuous lines of more than 1,000 miles to El Paso.

First to arrive on this busy scene (May 13, 1881) was the Southern Pacific, and a few days later came the Atchison & Topeka, a few months later the Texas & Pacific, and a few months later still the Galveston, Harrisburg & San Antonio. In the meantime the construction of the Mexican Central southward to the city of Mexico had begun, and was being pushed with the same energy that had characterized the building of these roads, all of which are now completed, and are parts of great competitive systems, connecting us with the world on every hand.

To-day, then, we have five railroads; a city of 5,500 people, with all the elements of wealth, progress, prosperity, and happiness, such as schools, churches, street railways, water works, gas works, electric light works, banks, building associations, a Federal court and custom house, telegraphs and telephone, sampling works, transfer company, fine hotels and public buildings, a public park, a city band and theater, a first-class fire department, fine residences and business houses, an excellent city government ; law, order, morality, good society ; an ice factory, union stock yards ; one daily and three weekly newspapers, one Live Stock and Mining Journal; a large and increasing commercial business with Mexico and the surrounding country, which is tributary to El Paso for a radius of 400 miles ; the county seat, with a court house and jail that will meet the ambitious demands of the county for the next twenty years, at least.

The superior and perhaps unequaled advantages of the city of El Paso, for reasons some of which have already been mentioned, and all of which we hope to demonstrate further on in this work, have caused the city to outstrip in its growth the surrounding country. The consequence is, that notwithstanding there are not less than 1,000,000 acres of alluvial valley, as fertile and productive as can be found on the continent,—enough to support in comfort half a million of people,—all of which, when settled, must look to this city as its commercial and political metropolis, and will add immensely to its stability, wealth, and advancement, we are now sending out of this city alone not less than $1,000,000 annually for the purchase of flour, hay, grain, pork, lard, butter, fruits, and vegetables, staples all of which can be produced here in great abundance and variety, and of a quality equal to any, and under the most favored conditions ; for it must be remembered that we not only have a soil of extreme fertility, capable of producing crops continually without the use of fertilizers, but our climate is adapted to the growth of a greater variety of products, either of fruits, cereals, or vegetables, than elsewhere, except under the same conditions of soil, latitude, and altitude, and so healthy and pleasant that there is not a day in the whole year in which man or beast cannot work out of doors without fear of danger or discomfort.

These facts—as to the capabilities of our soil, adaptability of our climate, cheapness of our lands, and numerous advantages of market, location, transportation, and communication, and the many pleasant and favorable conditions under which life may be maintained— have all been demonstrated to such a degree of success and certainty that we no longer hesitate to say to the intending immigrant, wherever he may be, whether he be farmer, stock raiser, capitalist, dairyman, manufacturer, miner, prospector, speculator, merchant, tourist, or health seeker, that these pages are dedicated to him; that the time has come when we know it to be our duty to *him*, as well as duty and pleasure to ourselves, to invite and urge him to read these pages, in which we will treat each special subject applicable to our country and situation in a plain, practical, truthful manner, with a view of interesting and informing him, so that he may not only know how and where he can probably better his own condition, by participating in and enjoying the advantages and benefits to which we invite him, but that he may thereby contribute his share to the general prosperity, wealth, and happiness that must surely result from the settlement and cultivation of this valley, the occupation of our vast areas for grazing, the development of our mineral resources, the embracing of our opportunities for manufacturing, the stimulation of our trade and commercial relations, the enjoyment of our fine scenery, salubrious air, health and life-giving atmosphere and climate; taking heed of our natural location and advantages, from which a great city must inevitably arise, to turn an honest penny by trading and speculating upon our prospects, to advance and invest capital upon our securities and in our property; to not only stop forever the outflow of our wealth, to the amount of a million annually, for flour, hay, grain, etc., as already mentioned, but to turn the tide in our favor by exporting these and other products, to the amount of millions; in short, to join the procession, and place ourselves under conditions where the road to prosperity is not only shorter, smoother, safer, and in all respects better than any we have ever known, or to which we have been invited, either by publications similar to this, or in any other manner. There is a chance here for everybody with either brains, energy, or capital, and for the happy possessor of all these there is an illimitable field; and they are invited to come.

As we have already illustrated in a general way, the physical geography, or rather the topography, of this particular locality (the City of El Paso and its immediate surroundings) is remarkable, and of such a nature as to give it a commanding importance in respect to trade, commerce, and military and political affairs; so much so that, we believe, greatness will be thrust upon it—that it must become the commercial and political metropolis of the Southwest. Nature has given her the position, and the laws of trade are as immutable as those of nature. The finger of destiny seems to point unerringly toward this supremacy.

This place is reached through a series of natural passes in the several chains or groups of mountains which lie across our paths here in every direction, east, west, north, south; and this city is itself located at the lower extremity of the most remarkable of all these gateways through nature's great barriers. One of these great chains of mountains was thrown by nature from east to west directly across the path of the "Rio Bravo del Norte" (the brave river of the North), as the Mexicans call it, on its course to the sea, and the great mountain was penetrated, subdued, conquered, by the "Brave River of the North;" and now it passes (as it has for untold ages)—or rather, it sweeps majestically, angrily, growlingly—through the great mountain, still making, as it has made in the past, a smooth and peaceful highway for commerce with Mexico, all of Northwestern Texas, Eastern Arizona, and Southern New Mexico.

Commerce is the weapon, the all-powerful arm, with which we have entered in earnest, and with every prospect of success, upon our conquest of Mexico,—a conquest not like that of Hernando Cortez, or Scott, or Taylor, yet we shall enter the halls of the proud Montezumas in greater triumph and return with a far richer reward than they, and with no stain or suspicion of wrong or oppression upon our consciences. We shall conquer Mexico with our arts of peace, our commerce; and El Paso will be the great highway through which it must be accomplished. And we will be richer, and Mexico both happier, richer, and more powerful, after she is thus subdued. Already both we and they are feeling the power and the beauty and glory of the coming of this winged goddess of peace, as she nestles lovingly here and flies swiftly there, freighted with kind messages and the arts of peace and progress. The railroad, the telegraph, these are the potent agencies of our gentle goddess; with these she subjugates, civilizes, enriches, and builds up the waste places. The entire railroad and telegraph systems of the continent are here united; and thus are we in communication and commercial intercourse not only with Mexico, but of the world, through all the cities and ports of Mexico as well as our own. Our trade with Mexico is daily assuming greater proportions, and, considering our great competitive system of railroads, and other advantages already mentioned, we believe that our business relations with Mexico alone will build up and sustain a large and important city here. At the same time our social relations are daily becoming more cordial and pleasant. The barriers of distrust and suspicion engendered by past misunderstandings, and fostered by foreign intrigues and interests, are fast melting away and disappearing before the benign influence of this knowledge of each other and each other's aims and aspirations, acquired from this interchange of ideas, courtesies and commodities. We are beginning to think better of the Mexican people and their country, and they are thinking better of us. We are beginning to understand each other, and there is no better way to understand men or nations than to trade with them. And Mexico is now fairly started on the high road to permanent peace and prosperity. She has now the most powerful as well as the most liberal and enlightened executive and government she has ever had. President Diaz, of whom we speak, is the father of the great projected railway system of Mexico, and essentially, and avowedly, the friend of progress as represented by Americans. So that from Mexico alone we have much to hope and nothing to fear; and this relation, Mexico is beginning to understand, is entirely reciprocal.

In addition to our reasonable expectations as to the importance of our geographical situation and commercial relations with Mexico, we have also reason to believe that the day is not far distant when we will be able to permanently command the entire trade of Northern Texas, Southern New Mexico and Eastern Arizona.

In fact, we have commanded that trade for the past year. We have been selling goods to all that portion of the country, and goods that were hauled past their own doors, then purchased here and shipped back to them, cheaper than they could lay them down direct from any other point. The competition in railroad freights has been so sharp to this point, where the roads terminate, and to which through rates were made, that all kinds of freights, regardless of quantity or class, from all competing points, such as Kansas City, St. Louis, New Orleans, and San Francisco, have been laid down here for 40 cents per 100 lbs; while to all points east and north, or anywhere on the lines of these roads, local rates prevailed, or rates one, two, three, four, and even five times as high as to this point. Simply because there was no competition, we have been selling the same goods to those points that were hauled past their doors. And, further, there is no doubt that this will become the point from which through and competitive rates will be made on cattle, ores, hay, grain, and all the products of this country, to all other points where there is competition. Therefore, and necessarily, these products will come here from long distances for shipment. There can be no question of the future of this place in this regard. It is inevitable, and we have no hesitation in calling the attention of the capitalist, merchant and speculator to these facts. Investigation will verify them, and that investigation we invite. The reader will, we hope, not fail to note also what must be the effect on the cost of living at a point where railroads are in competition, and where rates are so low.

In considering this whole question it must be remembered that the railroads were not attracted here to avail themselves of any business or trade that already existed; they came solely because of these facts of topography, physical geography, and the resulting laws of commerce which we have mentioned, and they will be the great instrumentalities of our glory and greatness. They will be, they are, the popular vehicle of a very large proportion of that commerce between the two worlds heretofore carried over the Isthmus, the seas and other routes.

But aside from all this, and aside from our own ex-

ports and imports, the local traffic will be considerable
and important, and will occasion tap railways in every
direction; for there will have to be transported, of our
own products, ores in large quantities to this point,
where they may be reduced; wood and coal to the mines
and to our reduction works, and other manufactories;
timber, lumber, iron, building material, etc, to the mines
and mills; breadstuffs, fruits, vegetables from the valley
to the mines and grazing lands, and live stock to the
markets; marble, granite, onyx, gypsum, sand, and other
like material, and innumerable other articles which enter
into the list of necessities and luxuries of American life,
and a great many new products peculiar to this combination of latitude and elevation.

AGRICULTURE AND HORTICULTURE.

That the valley of the Rio Grande, especially in the vicinity of El Paso, affords all the requisites, and therefore
is well adapted to the delightful and profitable pursuits of the agriculturist and horticulturist, no intelligent
citizen of this community need be told. Indeed, it has
become a fact so abundantly and perfectly demonstrated
that we wish now to announce it to the world, if possible,
in an authoritative manner.

To attain great perfection, and to achieve the most
considerable degree of success in these pursuits, favorable conditions of both soil and climate must be found.
We claim that those conditions exist here to as great, if
not greater, degree than can be found elsewhere on this
continent. Nearly all the products of the temperate
zone can be produced here in abundance and perfection. The cereals, wheat, corn, oats, barley, rye, etc.,

yield as much per acre, and of as good quality, as in any part of the United States.

The grasses—alfalfa, millet, timothy, bermuda, and all others which have been thus far introduced, do well. The Smyrna millets, grown here for the first time last year as a test, in small quantity, and under the most favored conditions, attained a growth, in two cuttings, of ten feet. It is estimated that it will yield from three to four tons per acre. This is a perennial of vigorous root and growth, spreads rapidly, runs deep, and is, therefore, well adapted to our soil.

Alfalfa was, we believe, first introduced into this vicinity by the late Gen. Magoffin, in 1849. It does remarkably well. May be cut from three to four times each season, aggregating four to six tons per acre, and two to four feet in height. This is also a perennial, with a vigorous growth of root, penetrating to as great a depth as thirteen feet, showing great adaptability to a dry climate. From present appearances, it would seem that this is destined to be the staple grass crop of the valley. It is very productive, hardy and tenacious of life, the best of food for cattle, horses, hogs and chickens, and has already become quite an important and remunerative industry.

Bermuda grass, wherever planted, indicates its love for our soil and its determination to stay. Its myriad rootlets permeate the soil and form an almost impenetrable sward. It is peculiarly adapted to lawns, parks, etc., and fills exactly that much-needed and desirable quality here.

Vegetables of nearly every known class and variety, and especially all those that are grown on vines, such as the melon, squash, pumpkin, etc., do as well here, in all respects, as in any part of the United States. The El Paso onion is already justly famous above all others.

Under the head of pomology, it may be said that our

soil and climate are perfectly adapted to the growth of apples, pears, peaches, plums, apricots, grapes, quinces, nectarines, almonds, **pecans,** prunes, and many others, such as strawberries, raspberries, gooseberries, too numerous to mention. All of these have been thoroughly tested; in fact, it is no longer a matter of experiment with any of them. They can be produced here in abundance and perfection.

While adapted to the growth of all kinds of grapes, the old "Mission grape," of dark purple hue, widely known now (and as distinctively as the El Paso onion), under the name of the "El Paso grape," is grown here in great perfection, and is a very superior grape for the table and for the manufacture of wine, brandy and raisins. An acre, with one thousand good vines, is worth here $1.000. A large quantity of these grapes (some 10,000 baskets), will be shipped this year to Eastern markets, yielding, no doubt, a satisfactory remuneration.

The superiority of our soil and climate for the growth of fruit is further shown by the fact that trees of the staple fruits, such as apples, pears and peaches, set out only two years since, are now bearing.

Flowers and shrubs of all kinds find here a natural and congenial home. Our alkaline soils can be utilized by growing any of the great varieties of the sugar beet, to which these soils seem singularly adapted. The cabbage and onion also thrive just as well in such soils; and in a few years of such cultivation, especially if manure is used, the alkali will be absorbed, and the land found suitable to the growth of anything grown elsewhere in the valley.

Small farms for the individual are preferable to large ones, unless there be a community of interest in all the people of a settlement. The land can be doubly cropped each year, so that one acre here answers as well as two further north. Every acre can and should be made a perfect

garden, and it will give support to a human being.
While agents for colonies are running hither and thither
seeking for locations, they should look to the valley lying in this favored climate, where lands are cheap, and
on the lines of railway. Time, in this case, is most
surely money in the pockets of the first comers.

THE EL PASO GRAPE.

The arable land of this county, and particularly of
this valley, is, as we have shown, admirably adapted to
agriculture, but most perfectly to the El Paso grape.
Those experienced in the cultivation of the vine, report
that all the conditions of the soil—humidity and temperature—are united here to produce the grape in the
greatest perfection. The soil, composed of disintegrated
matter of the older rocks and volcanic ashes, is light,
porous and rich. The frosts in the winter are just sufficiently severe to destroy the insects without injuring the
plant, and the rain seldom falls in its season when the
plant is flowering, or when the fruit is coming into ma-
turity and liable to rot from exposure to humidity. As
a consequence of these conditions, the fruit, when ripe,
has a thin skin, scarcely any pulp, and is devoid of the
musky taste so frequent with American grapes. Yearly
new vineyards are coming into bearing, counting their
vines by the thousand, while the production of wine is
becoming annually more and more an article of commerce and profit. Here may be found, and often in
great perfection, both the light white and red wines of
the Rhine and Bordeaux, and the heavier Burgundy,
port, sherry, and, with sufficient age, even a good Ma-
deira, with a grape acclimated by two hundred years of
cultivation, unexcelled for richness and lusciousness of
flavor, always free from blight and disease of every kind,
so destructive to European vineyards, so fatal to wine

growing on the Atlantic slope, and often so damaging even to California. With a soil and water as rich as that of the Nile, with an abundance of water for irrigation, and with sunny days and dewless nights, increasing in strength as the summer heats increase, the wines of the Rio Grande Valley promise to become as varied and as excellent as those of France or Spain.

RAISINS.

There is every reason to believe that this valley will become at no remote day a famous raisin district, perhaps more so than any on this continent. The soil and climate are peculiarly adapted to one of the best varieties of raisin grapes in the world. It is well known that raisins, to possess lasting qualities and best flavor, must be dried in the sunshine, then passed through the sweating process, and packed. And there is, perhaps, no place in America where the climate will so certainly and readily admit of this process as here; because at the period of closing the labors of the vineyard, the atmosphere is perfectly dry and clear, with scarcely a cloud upon the horizon for months. The best raisin in the world is made from the Muscat grape, of Egypt, and is cured and packed in just such an atmosphere as this. Our grape, the " El Paso grape." and this raisin industry that will certainly grow out of it, should attract the attention of those skilled in this art, and we trust this article may be read and noted by them carefully.

LIVE STOCK AND GRAZING.

This portion of the country, for hundreds of miles in every direction, outside of the great alluvial and agricultural valley of the Rio Grande, of which we have just written, consists of plains, uplands, and mountains, and having an altitude of from 3,500 to 7,000 feet, is admirably adapted to stock raising. The climate is everything that could be desired — mild, equable, healthy. Free from the effects of cold storms, of drouth, of disease, with none of the enemies which are so destructive to many of the cattle districts of the West and Southwest, there are here all the conditions that favor the rapid increase and growth of cattle, horses, sheep, and other live stock. The grasses are of great variety and peculiar excellence, due to the elevation above the sea, which gives life, vitality, and coolness to the atmosphere. There is no reason why the percentage of increase should not here reach the maximum. These are, we believe, justly considered the best breeding grounds for live stock on the continent. The loss from climatic causes is absolutely nothing. The new-born calf is as safe here in midwinter as in summer, and cattle are never drifted or driven from their ranges by the violence of the storms of any kind. Northers and sleet are unknown. We have often seen fat beef shipped to the eastern markets from these ranges in midwinter and early spring—February, March, and April. The shipments met with favor and profit; and the changes of condition in cattle, as between winter and summer, is, perhaps, less here than on any portion of the continent. The topography of the country is such, that the shelter and drainage are perfect. The grasses are greener, sweeter, and more nutritions in the higher altitudes in and around the mountains,

and the cattle in better condition. There is no question,
that the mountain ranges, will, at all seasons of the year,
afford the best of beef. The facilities for marketing stock,
procuring supplies, labor, etc. for the ranch, are excellent, probably none better are to be found. A great
competitive system of railroads centers here, hauling
empty cars eastward, and low rates can be obtained. In
fact, all the conditions exist here, for the successful
breeding and fattening of live stock, and for making El
Paso the center of an immense live stock interest, cover-
ing all of Northern Mexico, Western Texas, Southern
New Mexico, and Eastern Arizona.

The only drawback to the business is the scarcity of
water. About two-thirds of this great grazing country is
without natural water, and in order to make this vast
region available, it will be necessary to resort to wells,
wind-mills, reservoirs, and other artificial means. While
these are not as good in all respects as natural waters,
they have some peculiar and important advantages. By
enclosing these artificial wells, the cattle can be made
tame and gentle, not only adding to their flesh and value,
but greatly diminishing the cost of herding, handling, and
shipping, but they will locate more easily and permanently; and such ranges will not be encroached upon
by others, to any extent at all equal to those located on
natural waters. In fact, there are no reasons why the
ranges supplied with water by artificial means are not
quite as desirable, even more so, than those located on
natural waters. A little enterprise and capital will soon
overcome these apparent difficulties, and some of the best
ranges in the world will be had at a minimum cost; for
the price of these dry lands is very low indeed, particularly in Northern Mexico. The difference in price in
favor of the dry lands will, no doubt, more than pay the
cost of artificially obtaining abundant supplies of water.
Life and property are as much respected and as safe

over all this region, including Northern Mexico, as in
any of the Western States or Territories.

All these favorable conditions will be found to exist
here, and we have no hesitation in inviting all men interested in this great question to come and examine for
themselves. They will find vast vacant areas covered
with an abundance of nutritious food, to which perfect
titles can be acquired, a mild, equable climate, first-class
facilities for market, security, and every requisite and
element necessary to success. A branch of the "National
Live Stock Association" is located here, and is also do-
ing good work and arousing considerable interest in
Northern Mexico.

Live stock and lands in Mexico are exempt from tax-
ation.

In short, it may be said, that for the profitable raising
of horses, mules, cattle, sheep, and goats on an extensive
scale, no portion of the world can rival this district. Its
mild climate presents no rigors, while its mountain slopes,
valleys, and plains, are unlimited ranges of excellent
pasturage. The grasses of these plains and slopes are
by no means the least of nature's wonders. The "gram-
ma" and "mesquite" varieties, which most abound,
have a peculiar tenacity of life, and survive a succession
of dry seasons, and when apparently dead a few showers
will bring them out in full freshness; indeed, they change
from a single shower. These grasses are sweet and nu-
tricious, dry or green, and cattle thrive and fatten on
them. They cure on the ground before the coming of
the frost, making a natural hay. The natural configuration of this vast region is not the least of the many desirable advantages it presents. Situated as it is, from
4,000 to 7,000 feet above the level of the sea, fanned by
the purest atmosphere, giving a cool, refreshing and salubrious climate, pure and healthy water, the succession
of mountain and valley affords the most ample defence

against the heat of summer, as well as the storms of winter, which, however, are so little to be dreaded that artificial protection, shelter, or food of any kind, is wholly unnecessary, and is never provided. Our mesas (table lands), mountain gorges, and many portions of our plains, are most prolific in a variety of herbage suitable for all classes of animals, but especially for sheep. During the winter they afford a supply of pasturage so abundant that no additional food is required. By constant and steady supply of proper food by which the secretory powers are retained in full action, the uninterrupted increase of meat and fat in animals, and of growth of wool on sheep, is promoted; while cases of constipation and various diseases, frequently fatal in the States, by reason of sudden changes of food, are unknown here. There is not a day in the year in which cattle and sheep cannot find here sufficient food of a proper kind to keep their digestive organs in a healthy condition. Untold wealth is going to waste here every year, because our grasses are not consumed—a wealth that will prove greater than our vast mineral deposits. The one we have *in* the earth, the other we have the means of producing *on* the soil. Come, then, and gather some of this wealth from the surface, by providing means to consume these grasses—a most pleasant and profitable business under such conditions as are to be found here.

No intelligent man need be told that the raising of live stock is profitable. We will only point to its history during the past ten years. Nothing has ever equaled it in results. It must always remain a good business. More money has been made in cattle during the past ten years than in any other business that can be named. And the raising of sheep and horses has also been very remunerative.

3

MINES AND MINERALS.

There can be no question that there is mineral wealth in nearly all of our surrounding mountains, for hundreds of miles in **every direction.** Thousands of good prospects **have been** found in the Organs, **the** Jarillas, the San Andres, **the** Guadalupe, the Quitman, the Chenati and Eagle Mountains, constituting the groups nearest to El Paso, and forming **a** background to the great picture of which El Paso is both the focus and radiating **point.** In the Organs, several of these prospects can now fairly be called mines. They have reached a stage of consid**erable develo**pment and are worked with profit, shipping **their ores to Denver and** Pueblo, Colorado, or to Socorro or Kingston, **New Mexico, for** reduction. Many others are in process of development, and are dumping their ores upon the ground, awaiting the advent of a railroad, or reduction works. **Several** promising discoveries have been made within **a few** miles of this city. There are, no doubt, hundreds of these prospects that can be worked **with** profit the moment the questions of transportation **and** reduction are solved satisfactorily, so that the profits **may** not be consumed in these processes. All of this applies with equal force to that vast portion of Northern Mexico **of** which El Paso is already, and must always remain, the business center.

In fact, there seems to be **no end to** the mineral wealth of this country, far and near, in every direction; and one cannot but be amazed in contemplating the results which must follow its development. Scarcely **a** day passes **that we do not hear of** some discovery within this scope **of country.**

Coal has **also** been discovered on three sides. North, 150 miles, is the White Oaks deposit, west 150 is the Corralitas deposit, and southeast, 100 miles, the Eagle

Springs deposit, only four miles from the Galveston, Harrisburg & San Antonio Railway. The quality of this coal is excellent, particularly the White Oaks deposit, which is pronounced to be inferior to none in the world.

All of this great mineral district has been retarded in its development by the lack of capital, not only to work the mines, but to furnish cheap transportation, cheap fuel and reduction and smelting works. The question of transportation is now partially solved by the railroads already constructed and centering here; and with present facilities there is no doubt of the capacity of the districts now being worked, and where railroad facilities are within reach, to supply this city with sufficient ore to cause it to begin to assume the importance of a center for smelting and reduction works, which we are satisfied it must inevitably do; for it must be borne in mind, in considering such a statement, that we have unequaled railroad facilities, where there will always be more or less competition, both in hauling coal, the most important factor, and in hauling the ores. These ores contain the necessary fluxes for smelting readily and cheaply.

That mining as a business will pay, it is only necessary for us to point to the statistics and history concerning it, as shown in California, Nevada, Utah, Colorado, Wyoming and Montana. Such progress has been made, both in the art and science of mining, that under like conditions of management there is no reason why it should not be classed as one of the legitimate pursuits, with every essential element of safety and success.

There are also large deposits of salt in the eastern portion of the county, about ninety miles from El Paso, from which great quantities of an excellent, pure salt is taken.

Limestone is also found in great abundance, from which the best of lime is made. Several kilns are established near the city.

Large beds of clay also abound, from which an excellent quality of brick is made; tiling and a coarse variety of ware is made from it also. The Organ Mountains also furnish kaolin, the substance from which fine china and porcelain are made.

Marble of a very fine and superior quality has also been discovered in several localities, not far from El Paso, and will soon be quarried, profitably no doubt.

A deposit of the beautiful Mexican onyx has also been lately discovered and located a few miles northwest of the city.

One of the largest known deposits of gypsum, of the variety known as anhydrite, much resembling granulated sugar, does not require calcining, and when ground makes an excellent hydraulic cement, is situated about seventy miles north of El Paso; is twenty by sixty miles in extent, and is open for location, and, no doubt, will some day prove of value.

Building stone of several kinds, and in great quantity, lies almost within the city limits, and is abundant everywhere near the mountains. Among those that abound are limestone, granite and sandstone.

An important feature of the mines in this vicinity is that the prospects are generally sufficiently rich from the very surface to pay the working expenses; and, where this ore can be reduced, there is no reason why the work should not progress. The mines are, as a rule, situated at high altitudes, and the formation is not permeated with water, there being no snow at this altitude sufficient either to permeate the formation or prevent work at any and all times. The danger of caving and necessity for timbering throughout is avoided. All of which adds materially to the profits. To the capitalist, miner and prospector, we would say, Come, here is a field worthy of your attention.

IRRIGATION.

ITS HISTORY, INTRODUCTION INTO AMERICA, AND PRESENT ASPECT.

The greatest prerequisite to success in agriculture, fruit-raising, etc., in the Western States and Territories, is water. A constant and abundant supply of water is the true key to Western progress and development. In nearly all of that country the rainfall is totally insufficient, and not to be relied upon; hence Western people have been forced to study the problem of irrigation. Having been forced to look into this question, we naturally try to trace up its origin and history.

The system found in California and in this country has been bequeathed to us by Mexico, and was inherited by them from Spain. Looking farther back, we find that it was one among the many good gifts which the Moors gave to Spain when they overran that country in the 8th century. Whether the Moors obtained it direct from the Arabs, or took it from the Egyptians, we are unable to determine at this late day. But in inquiring after its still more ancient origin and source, we must not stop this side of the valleys of the Euphrates and Tigris. If we start here, in the dim and shadowy ages of antiquity, beyond which even tradition becomes unintelligible, we will find that, with few exceptions, the highest types of civilization and the brightest examples of progress and prosperity have been located, sustained and nurtured by systems of irrigation.

A FEW PERTINENT EXAMPLES.

The glory, grandeur and wealth of royal Babylon, of Nineveh, Thebes, Bagdad, Cairo and Memphis, around which, as common centers, the civilization of great periods of time hung and radiated, were all attributable to and dependent upon the agricultural perfection surrounding them, and made possible by irrigation. We might go further, and say that it has been the support and sustenance of the civilized world long after the cessation of Roman sway. For none will fail to recognize that the Nile country alone supported what was known as the Roman world, and that Egypt was always regarded as the granary of the empire. The Egyptian people were overthrown and vanquished, but their system of irrigation survived and gave sustenance to Roman civilization, and remained intact throughout all the vicissitudes and changes. If anything, irrigation was better in the days of Semiramis than in the days of Boabdil, although, like the other concomitants of the beautiful Alhambra, orchards, vineyards and meadows, as then seen along the banks of the Guadalquiver, speak of a splendid development, both material and intellectual. The Moors obtained from their Arab progenitors a taste for astronomy and some inclination toward practical mathematics, and to some extent we find applied mathematics in its crude state assisting in making large portions of their country bloom and blossom as the rose by the ingenious devices which the Moors had of supplying water to the gardens, orchards, vineyards and beautiful meadows which dotted old Hispania during their occupancy.

It is a fact which cannot be controverted, that after the reconquest of Spain and the expulsion of the Moriscoes, Spain began to decline. The splendid schools of Granada, and the numerous manufactories of Valencia and other places, gradually faded away and left Spain without any support, save that which she gathered by the sword, for she had neglected almost entirely her irrigation system; and the apology for one which we have, and which was found in California when that State was acquired, is the system handed down by the successors of those Spaniards who vanquished and expelled the Moriscoes from Spain.

A NEW SYSTEM NEEDED.

It is our purpose now to show the inadequacy of this system, and the present results of it, as compared with the capabilities and possibilities of a new system which the progressive American demands and will have. We have touched but very briefly upon its antiquity, for the reason that four-fifths, we might even say nine-tenths of English-speaking people are practically unacquainted with this system. Their civilization, comparatively speaking, is in its infancy; it is still jejune, and has grown up in a climate of moisture and regular rainfall, and operating upon what might be termed virgin soil, and until recently the people of the United States had no necessity of irrigation. But times are changing, and the time will come when four-fifths of the population of America may be dependent upon irrigation in their agricultural pursuits. Then, we say, we will do well to look into this question, and when the American idea once takes hold of it, systems new and prolific will evolve wonderful results.

Having brought the reader down to the consideration of this point, we make the broad statement that the results of irrigation in California, Colorado, Arizona and New Mexico show, in a large majority of instances, an increase of one hundred per cent. over results dependent upon rainfall alone in the Eastern and Middle States. The history of the West proves our statement to be correct. This once admitted, then here in the valley of the Rio Grande the soil, the climate and the water must cause the reader to stop and investigate, with renewed and eager interest, the conditions and statements which we place before them.

THE AMERICAN NILE.

Our Rio Grande is the American Nile. The similarity is complete—the analogy remarkable. The Nile has its source in an interior plateau—the Alps of Abyssinia, many of which are covered in their winter time by heavy masses of snow. The lower portions of the great plateau are visited during April by perfect deluges of rain, such as only tropical countries can produce. The accumulation of these torrential rains, and the melting of the Alpine snows, causes the river to rise with almost clock-like regularity between the first and fifth days of May, and by the end of that month it is booming and bank full. The turbid floods go tearing their way through rough defiles and deep cañons that fissure a volcanic country, the formation of which, travelers tell us, is very much like that of Colorado, with limestone, granite, and occasional vast trachyte formations predominating. The waters become thoroughly charged with a combination of mineral ingredients, which contain in themselves all the elements of fertility. When the turbid floods reach the great valley of Nubia and Egypt they are of a slimy consistence, and about the beginning of June, just before the annual planting time begins in that country, they commence to overflow their banks and spread over the valley lands, which have been in a state of cultivation ever since Abraham's time, and probably long before. Whatever the crops of the preceding year may have abstracted from the soil is more than restored by the abundant deposit of fertile mud which the river leaves behind when its period of boom is over. The lands are found covered with a crust of stiff slime, containing lime, potash, chlorides, ammonia, and various other valuable ingredients. Into this rich slime the

Egyptian fellah casts his seed, and in an incredibly short time, with scarcely any cultivation, and only such subsequent and additional irrigation as the reservoirs filled during the river's rise will allow, he reaps more than an hundred fold. No manure is ever applied, but the soil is constantly getting richer, and bears at the present day, after a thousand years of neglect and mismanagement, better crops than in the days of the Pharaohs and Ptolemies.

THE NILE'S STEP-BROTHER.

High up on the interior plateau of Southern Colorado, in the legendary country of San Juan, among wild crags and heaven-aspiring battlements covered with eternal snow, rises the Rio Grande, or as the Spaniards, who must have seen it first some time in May or June, called it, the Brave River of the North. It rises in the great porphyritic formation of the San Juan, near Ouray and Lake City, and is fed by the immense snow masses that almost constantly cover that inhospitable country. It tears its way out like a young giant, grinding the rocks to pieces as it goes along, and becomes surcharged with their mineral constituents, identically the same that the waters of the Nile contain, and only adding an immense quantity of aluminoid detritus, which makes it muddier even than "Old Muddy," the Missouri itself. The similarity of the chemical constituents of the two kinds of water has often been noted by scientific travelers and experts. Both, after being allowed to settle, show a liquid of limpid purity, and of remarkably pleasant taste and wholesome character. But in their native turbulency, both are equally muddy, and leave the same thick sediment of slimy mud behind, after their waters recede from an overflow. This takes place with our Rio Grande usually in May and June, when the immense snow masses of the San Juan country begin to melt. Then the

river plays some fantastic pranks, occasionally overflowing its banks from foot-hill to foot-hill.

These amiable eccentricities will have to be curbed
when the population of the valley becomes denser and
more Americanized. Judicious rip-rapping at exposed
angles, and a general planting of the banks with willows
and Bermuda grass, and the building of the great canal,
will prevent overflows except by means of the irrigating
channels.

This annual rise of our Rio Grande begins at the very
time when irrigation becomes necessary—immediately
when ready for the plough and the seed. It continues
during June and July, and usually lasts long enough to
tie on to the rainy season of July and August.

The system of ditches is at present badly planned and
very inadequate for the purpose intended. The acequia
madre which supplies Paso del Norte with water is about
as good a specimen of an irrigating ditch, planned and
executed by Mexican labor only, as we can find in the
valley. There is at present scarcely any systematic attempt along the whole course of the river, from the northern boundary of New Mexico down to where the cañon
country below the mouth of the Concho River commences,
to construct suitable dams below the points where it is
intended to take out acequias, and thus obtain a full
head and a constant supply of water at a comparatively
trifling expense. All these points will come to be better
understood and executed after a while, when a pushing
and energetic American population occupies the valley
and converts its fertile but now unused lands into vineyards and orchards.

The construction of a great irrigating canal, such as is
in contemplation at the present time, to extend from El
Paso to near Camp Rice, demands naturally a large outlay of labor and material. To repay this outlay, all the
waters so taken out must be used to advantage, and large

tracts of land must thus become dependent upon the one great canal. No single farmer, and no single neighborhood, can undertake such a task. Co-operative labor must be organized, or capital be induced to assist and take hold.

THE VALLEY IRRIGATING CANAL.

Our readers will pardon us if we again refer to this subject, but its importance demands it. This canal once constructed, every acre within the valley will become a vineyard, an orchard, or meadow. All the idle water which flows wastefully to the Gulf, will be made to yield the greater part of its wealth of plant food which it holds in suspension, and we will no longer witness this great volume of water running past our doors while our ditches are dry, when they should be full to overflowing.

The flow of water in the Rio Grande is ample for the needs of the valley. The opportunity is here offered to the capitalist to make a profitable investment in an enterprise which will give a richer return than can be found elsewhere in this country. The cost of a canal from El Paso to Camp Rice, a distance of 53 miles, has been estimated to be approximately $250,000. There would be tributary to such a canal some 150,000 acres of valley land, ready for cultivation as soon as water can be obtained. Every acre of this land would then contribute to the canal company a yearly stipend of say one dollar for water privileges, which would insure to the investors a net income of about $100,000 per annum. These facts and figures can be verified by personal investigation. Capital is now, for the first time in three years, beginning to look to the far West, and with restored confidence and abundant crops there is no point in the West which will command that attention which El Paso will command in the near future.

STATISTICAL AND SCIENTIFIC.

If the reader is not deterred by a few dry facts and prosaic figures, he will find it profitable to follow us with due patience a little while longer.

In a general way, the limit of agriculture, without irrigation is indicated by the curve of 20 inches rainfall, and where the rainfall is equally distributed throughout the year, this limitation is without exception. But in certain districts the rainfall is concentrated in certain months, so as to produce a "rainy season;" and wherever the temperature of the rainy season is adapted to the raising of crops, it is found that farming can be carried on with even a little less than 20 inches of annual rain. This, however, holds good only in certain portions of the United States. Nowhere in Texas are 20 inches of rain sufficient for agriculture, while in Dakota and Minnesota a much less amount is sufficient.

The annual rainfall in El Paso, as ascertained by a series of observations for a number of years (over twenty), has been found to be 8.53 inches. This precipitation is distributed generally in the following ratio: Spring, 0.43 inches; summer, 3.49 inches; fall, 3.38 inches; winter, 1.23 inches. Thus at a glance will be seen the utter hopelessness of carrying on agriculture of any kind in this section of country without artificial irrigation.

In comparison with the 8.53 inches of annual rainfall at El Paso we find 31.30 inches at San Antonio, 27.58 at New Braunfels, 33.52 at Austin, and 22.61 inches even at Fort Clark. At all of these places "dry farming" can be carried on, and ordinarily with profit and a reasonable share of certainty. But there will be occasional droughts or cloud-bursts, and sometimes a whole season's hard labor is lost to the patient husbandman without a particle of fault on his part. But how does the farmer,

gardener and orchardist stand in districts depending
upon irrigation ?

ADVANTAGES OF A SYSTEM OF IRRIGATION.

Crops cultivated by irrigation are not subject to the
vicissitudes of rainfall. The farmer fears no droughts ;
his labors are seldom interrupted, and his crops are
rarely injured by storms. This immunity from drought
and storms renders agricultural operations much more
certain and profitable than in regions of greater humidity. Again, the water comes down from the mountains
and plateaus freighted with fertilizing materials derived
from decaying vegetation and the soils of the upper regions, which are spread by the water used in irrigation
over the cultivated lands.

It may safely be anticipated that all the lands re-
deemed by irrigation in the Rio Grande valley will be
highly cultivated and abundantly productive, and agriculture will be but slightly subject to the vicissitudes of
scant and excessive rainfall. A stranger entering this
region for the first time is apt to conclude that the soil
is sterile, because of its chemical composition, but experience demonstrates the fact that all the soils are suitable for agricultural purposes when properly supplied
with water. Altogether the fact suggests that far too
much attention has heretofore been paid to the chemical
composition of soils, and too little to those physical conditions by which moisture and air are supplied to the
roots of the growing plants.

PRACTICAL AND THEORETICAL DETAILS.

The unit of water employed in irrigating enterprises
in the West is usually the inch,—meaning thereby the
amount of water that will flow through an orifice one

inch square. But in practice this quantity is very in-
definite, due to the "head," or amount of pressure from
above; in some districts this latter is taken at six inches.
Another source of uncertainty exists in the fact that
increase in the size of the orifice and increase in the
amount of flow do not progress in the same ratio. An
orifice of one square inch will not admit of a discharge
one-tenth as great as an orifice of ten square inches.
An inch of water, therefore, is variable with the size of
the stream as well as with the head or pressure. With
the influx of Americans into the Rio Grande Valley, it
will become necessary to adopt a more definite mode of
measuring irrigating water. In measuring the volume
of water which is carried down by a stream, it is usual
to state the number of cubic feet which the stream will
deliver per second.

This matter—ascertaining the amount of water flowing down the Rio Grande at different seasons of the year
—is one of exceeding importance in estimating the agricultural capacities of the valley, and it is unfortunate
that the task has never been performed in a thorough
and systematic manner. Some very valuable estimates
of the volume of water in the river were made some
thirty years ago, when the first official boundary line
between the two republics was run by Emory; but as
they were made at only one particular stage of the river,
and did not extend over the full period of a year, their
value in an investigation of this subject is only acci-
dental. Then again at Del Norte, not far from the head-
waters of the river, observations were made by the
Powell Geological Survey which were more systemat-
ically conducted, and extended over the different seasons
of the year, thus making them of some practical utility
for the agriculture of Colorado. But the case is so entirely altered away down at El Paso, that we have
practically no accurate observations to guide us in our

examination here. This is greatly to be regretted ; without these data we can only approximately deal with the irrigation problem.

In determining the amount of water carried by any particular stream which can be utilized for irrigating purposes, Powell has already pointed out that this quantity is variable in each stream from season to season and from year to year. He long ago pointed out that the irrigable season is but a portion of the year. To utilize the entire annual discharge of a river, it would be necessary to hold the surplus flowing in the non-growing season, in large reservoirs. But as such a disposition of the waters of the Rio Grande will be a matter of the undetermined future, the question of immediate practical importance is resolved into a consideration of the amount of water that it will afford during the irrigating season.

In May, June, and July the volume of water in the pass near Fort Bliss will average 300 feet in width and five in depth, with a velocity of five miles an hour ; in August, September, and October it will average 100 feet in width and two and a half to three feet in depth, with a velocity of two and a half miles per hour. When considered that by the 10th of July the requirements of irrigation for fruits is over, there will then be more than a sufficiency for the late vegetable and alfalfa crops.

It must not be forgotten that the composition of the soil throughout the Rio Grande Valley is such that the subsoil will hold water for weeks and even months, and gradually yields the absorbed moisture to the overlying soil by slow upward percolation, or capillary attraction, during the season when the growing crops require its fertilizing effects.

The foregoing remarks are of necessity of a merely desultory character. The subject of irrigation is among Americans a comparatively new one, and no great stock of reliable data relating to it has so far been accumulated. The object of the foregoing article is simply to call attention to the importance of the subject in connection with the settlement of the Rio Grande Valley by progressive and enlightened agriculturists—a settlement in which El Paso and the district of country tributary to it will always play the leading role.

SOCIETY, LAW AND ORDER.

The society in this city is mixed. Every element is represented, as well as almost every State and nationality; yet there is as great a proportion of refined and cultivated people here, in proportion to our population, as can be found in any Western city.

We have an excellent city and county government, and the laws are as good and as well enforced as in any city or county, excepting none, East or West. Life and property are as secure, values are as well established and maintained; and, with the good society, healthy and delightful climate, pretty and picturesque country and scenery, handsome and eligible location of the city as to drainage, etc., railroad, telegraph, and mail facilities with all parts of the world, educational, religious, and many other advantages which will be hereafter mentioned, make all, or nearly all, the conditions of life here both agreeable and pleasant. Kindness, hospitality, and frankness are now, as always, traits of the frontiersman. In the cabin, the dug-out, or in the mansion the stranger is welcomed; the neighbor finds a neighbor indeed. Nowhere will immigrants or strangers of any class find less jealousy, envy, or interference than here, and nowhere will they find a warmer welcome, kindness, sympathy, or material assistance. The thousands of new-comers, now citizens, assure this, associated as they are in social, commercial, moral, and religious objects. In politics, where naturally lines would be sharply drawn, there is absolutely no sectional distinction, and the county is about equally divided between the two parties. We will give all immigrants a hearty welcome, and extend to them full and complete protection. We have no prejudices to overcome, for we are already cosmopolitan.

NORTHERN ENERGY—HOW AFFECTED.

One subject, that of the effect of this climate on Northern energy, we thought we would dilate upon, but, on reflection, will only briefly allude to it. Most Northern people believe that our climate is oppressively warm in summer, and also imagine that white persons cannot labor, or at least do not ; that people who reside in this latitude have but little energy or industry, and that the Northern immigrant would soon lose his former ambition and activity. Now, we have given the temperatures of the seasons, which are conclusive as to the moderate heat, and the reasons why this climate invigorates, instead of depresses ; and we can confidently refer to the native-born citizens, and the earlier and later immigrants, as to continued sustained labor in the field, workshop, or office. It is true, we have in the Mexican population a class of indolent, shiftless people (the fault of their Indian blood), who live and subsist easier than they can in the North, as the soil produces easily and the climate is favorable ; but the person who has a desire to secure a home and competence can work here in more comfort, and employ more days profitably, than he can anywhere else.

4

SCHOOLS.

Great as are the manifold attractions offered by the climate, the soil, and other physical advantages of El Paso county and her tributary surroundings, none of them equal the advantages she will derive from the princely provision which the fathers of the republic made for the education of the millions of youth who will in the near future be numbered among her population. The far-sighted statesmanship of those who laid the foundation of the "Lone Star" Republic provided for the education of generations yet unborn, a more generous revenue than is enjoyed by the schools of any State in the American Union. Nay, more than this; as we read the page on which these princely revenues are dedicated to education, we shall see that neither Oxford nor Cambridge have such royal endowments as the sages of Texas gave to the university and schools of Texas.

There is a permanent school fund of $3,500,000. That of Massachusetts is only two-thirds as large. These lands have been set apart for educational purposes:

For a university	1,221,400 acres.
County school domain	2,833,920 "
Central school domain	50,000,000 "
Total	54,055,320 acres.

So much for the permanent support of the schools. Let us see what provision is made for their present maintenance, besides the interest on the $3,500,000 Permanent Fund. This is yielding an annual income of more than $200,000, and is increasing $100,000 a year from land sales. The Constitution sets apart more than one-fourth the general revenue of the State, and $1.00 poll-tax for the support of common schools. In the year 1880, and since then, this amounted to nearly $2,000,000 annually. Besides this amount, there is the interest on the County School Fund of $550,020.00, being the amount realized and invested by those counties which have sold their lands in whole or in part. In some cities an additional local tax is levied for the support of schools. The school lands of El Paso county, all of which are unsold, and are being held for a better figure, are now worth $75,000. So much for the provision for schools. What is being done with the money that is available now? Of course, in sparsely settled communities the inauguration of schools is difficult, and it is almost impossible to apply any strict system; there must be more or less flexibility. Free schools are maintained in more than 160 counties; these are attended by more than 200,000 children, and in them are employed more than 5,000 teachers. The State has also established two normal schools. At these schools the students are both educated and boarded free of charge. From these a supply of trained teachers is constantly going to all portions of the State. An agricultural college has also been erected by the State, at a cost of more than $200,000, and the college has since been endowed with 1,000,000 acres of land. Thus generously has Texas provided for the education of all classes of her youth. In El Paso county we have five public schools, four of which, those at Concordia, Ysleta, Socorro and San Elzario, are maintained wholly by these State endowments.

In the city of El Paso an additional local tax is levied for the support of schools. A fine school building was completed in the autumn of 1884, costing $20,000. The board of education consists of the best representative men of the city, and they have made the school an honor to the city, offering facilities for every grade of advancement, and no better advantages can be found elsewhere for a thorough preparatory college education. The system of instruction and course of study are both up with the most approved and most recent methods in operation.

The corps of teachers is of the best, and is under the direction of a superintendent of experience. The salaries paid teachers command the best talent in the profession; $75 per month is the minimum. A printed code of rules and regulations is in force which, in itself, shows the interest taken and results expected.

If our schools continue to improve and prosper as they have begun, El Paso will, ere long, be renowned for her educational advantages as she now is for business and other enterprises.

RELIGIOUS INSTITUTIONS AND PRIVILEGES.

The people of Texas are eminently a religious people. There is no State in the Union where church-going facilities are more highly prized, or where a larger proportion of citizens are members of church organizations; about three-quarters of a million of her people are recognized members of religious denominations; and this is fully borne out in regard to the city and county of El Paso. Surely a community in which one-third of the population profess direct church affiliations cannot be very lawless. Almost every denomination is represented here, both with churches, Sunday schools, pastors and membership, in a manner not excelled in any other city or county in the United States, of its age or population. And the immigrant or stranger will find here, outside of the churches, a strong and healthy moral sentiment, guiding and controlling the community, and the individual members thereof in all their acts.

TO THE INVALID.

This climate cannot be excelled for its sanitary qualities. The mercury has rarely been noted below 20° above, and then only for a few hours at a time. Snows seldom whiten the ground, and lie but a few hours. Damp, chilly days, and hot, sultry nights are unknown. The heat of summer is not oppressive, and sunstroke has never been known. The sky is clear the year round. No entire day has been known when the sun and stars have not been seen. The atmosphere is unsurpassed for its dryness and purity; full of electricity, it is wonderfully exhilarating, and never burdened with malarious or poisonous exhalations. Blankets or cover of some kind are necessary for all on nights which follow the hottest days, because the nights are cool, though not damp. Sleeping with doors and windows open, or in the open air, may be practiced with impunity. The asthmatic invalid or the consumptive may sit out of doors, ride or walk in the sunshine 350 days in the year with pleasure and comfort, and may always enjoy refreshing sleep at night; thus securing the most essential conditions for the restoration of a shattered nervous system and broken constitution.

Free and full breathing of pure air is the most important for a sufferer from diseases of the liver and lungs. Make such a person breathe, and he will live; whatever makes him breathe faster makes his blood flow more rapidly, and be better aerated. His appetite will increase, digestion and assimilation will respond to the increased action of the lungs, which is secured by the elevation of this valley. Here one must breathe more fully and more rapidly than nearer the sea level, and its air is as pure as any on the face of the earth. A perma-

ment increase of breathing capacity, caused by rarefied air,
prevents the formation of tubercles, and often heals
those already formed.   At this elevation (4,000 feet) this
increase is not so great as to be injurious, as is sometimes the case at higher elevations.   Such are some of
the conditions which give to this valley (in this locality)
an extremely healthy and invigorating climate, free from
the malaria of the hot, damp regions of the river beds and
low lands of the Southern States, and from the mountain
fevers, colds, influenzas, asthmas and consumptions of
the higher ranges of the Rocky Mountains, and cold,
fog-bound regions of the Northern States.   A more desirable climate cannot be found the world over.   Persons
shut out from the light of the sun are most disposed to
consumption.   For such, daily sunlight is everything.
This country, of which we write, has more sunny days
than any region of the United States, probably more
than *any* other place, and the invalid, therefore, cannot
but enjoy that benefit, unless he purposely excludes
himself from it.

WHAT PHYSICIANS SAY.

Florida and Cuba are warmer in winter, but they have
an atmosphere loaded with vapor, and winter is the
period of the greatest rains and, consequently, cloudy
days.   The invalid, seeking to regain health, will not go
to them if he follows the advice of Dr. Chambers, in
his Lectures on the Renewal of Life.   That eminent Eng-
lish physician says:

"In choosing a home for a consumptive, do not mind
the average height of the thermometer, or its variations:
do not trouble yourself about the mean rainfall; do not
be scientific at all; but find out by somebody's journal
how many days were fine enough to go out forenoon and
afternoon; that is the test you require; and by that you
may be confidently guided."

Tried by such a test, the invalid must locate here. Here is no rank, rich vegetation, saturated with moisture, and constantly undergoing decomposition. Vegetation dries up—never rots. Meat, stripped and hung in the open air and sun, in mid-summer, will cure, and is preserved without salt. Such air, when inhaled, gives a stimulus and vital force which can only be given by so pure an atmosphere. One having a predisposition to consumption comes to this valley and is immediately relieved. This altitude is not too high for the consumptive in any stage, except in the most extreme cases. And so with any organic disease of the heart. Any person with a fair constitution, who settles here, or near here, stands a better chance of enjoying a healthful life and of attaining his three score years and ten than in any other part of the Union. To the young of consumptive families, it offers special inducements. Here many a brilliant and useful life, which might otherwise be lost before reaching the meridian of manhood, may be prolonged to a vigorous old age.

Read the report of the committee of our physicians on Sanitarium, published below, upon which absolute reliance can be placed.

SANITARIUM.

The influence of climatic conditions is an important agent for favorably modifying the cause of various chronic diseases. There are few if any pulmonary affections or other chronic maladies which may not be either cured, suspended in their course, or relieved by the influence of judiciously selected climate. From the failure

of the materia medica to cope with this disease, attention
has been drawn to the modifying influence of climate
upon chronic pulmonary disorders. The conditions of
soil and atmosphere favorable to the development of
phthisis pulmonalis are well known. Damp, ill-drained
land, cold, humid air, sudden changes of temperature,
lack of sunlight, anti-hygienic surroundings—all contribute to depress the general health and to occasion the
fearful prevalence of consumption in low-lying districts
and in large cities. It is therefore evident that in the
search for a climate for the prevention and cure for consumption, dryness of air and soil and the invigorating
influences of sunlight must be substituted for the delete-
rious conditions of ground and atmosphere mentioned
above.

That climate is a potent agent in the prevention of
phthisis pulmonalis is demonstrated by the fact that a
region of comparative immunity from the disease is found
in high altitudes. It is therefore proposed to elucidate
some of the different factors which tend materially to
modify and counteract the effect of diseases in this climate, and the invalid tourist and immigrant cannot but
see the extraordinary advantages to be derived by settlement in our midst.

The latitude and longitude having been given heretofore, it is found that the elevation of El Paso, the county
seat of El Paso County, is near 4,000 feet, in round num-
bers, above sea level, and consists of an alluvial sandy
deposit, exceedingly porous, and possesses a great fac-
ulty of absorbing water and moisture. Small and large
ponds and marshes are notably absent: hence the fact,
in view of the altitude, that so little malaria or malarial
fevers are seen or known to complicate the ordinary pre-
vailing complaints among the inhabitants of the valley.

The river water is muddy, but settles readily, yielding
a pure and potable supply for every use. Wells are

driven with but little difficulty, and water clear as crystal is secured anywhere from seven to fifteen feet.

The physical conformation of land beyond the valley is diversified, being rolling mesas, broken foot-hills, and picturesque mountains. With the exception of the pass, El Paso is protected closely on the west, north and south by a main spur of the Rocky Mountains, and a slightly elevated plateau is on the east side, extending some sixty or seventy miles.

Owing to the exceedingly great porosity of the soil, humidity of the atmosphere is very insignificant, even after a considerable rainfall. The soil receives much of its moisture from below the surface, and in this way supplies, in a great measure, its needs in the growth of timber, grasses and vegetation. The paludial emanations of the soil, with little or no marshy lands or standing water, is so slight that the ordinary effects of malarial poisoning are rarely ever observed in one who has resided here any length of time.

It has been claimed that five or six thousand feet elevation furnishes an atmosphere superior to that of a higher or lower altitude, but such is not the case, for there are many conditions of the atmosphere, *per se*, such as degrees of moisture and dryness, temperature, relative velocity and general direction of wind, the natural surroundings, all make up the general salubriousness of the climate and better fit it for the invalid and consumptive. Other reasons why too great elevations above sea level should be avoided, is because of the too great aptitude to passive congestion of the lungs and heart, mountain fevers, cold, raw winds, inability too often of securing a sufficient variety of food and the ordinary comforts of a home life that may be had at lower altitudes. Altitude has a specially notable effect, inasmuch as there is a general increase in the bulk of the lungs and an enlargement of the chest of inhabitants

of elevated regions. It also produces large **dimensions**
of the air cells, enabling a freer discharge of accumulat-
ing secretions, permitting **larger** influx of pure **air,**
exercising a strongly antagonistic and germicidal influence, and rendering the lungs increasingly inapt to
take on a tubercularizing action. With the rise above
the sea level the air becomes rarefied and the atmospheric
pressure is considerably diminished. At the height of
4,000 feet the atmospheric pressure is about thirteen and
a half instead of fifteen pounds to the square inch, and
the proportion of oxygen is diminished twelve per cent.
This attenuation of the air produces important changes
in the economy.

The mechanical effect of the rarefied air is to increase
the frequency and depth of respiration and to accelerate
the pulse. A greater amount of air must be inhaled to
satisfy the demand for oxygen. Hence the lungs have a
tendency to be completely filled, the elastic tissue of the
vesicles is stretched and the thorax is expanded to its
fullest capacity. At moderate elevations the system
quickly adapts itself to the lessened atmospheric pressure, but when great heights are rapidly attained, as
with aeronauts, copious hemorrhages from the lungs
ensue. In the altitude of Denver hæmoptysis frequently
occurs in consumptives in the stage of excavation.

Dr. Denison says: "The lessened tension of the air,
and the increased frequency of respiration, force the
blood to pass more quickly through the lungs, and the
rapid and perfect renewal of capillary circulation is
opposed to the stages of early and chronic inflammation.
This improved capillary circulation, together with a
more perfect expansion of the thorax, loosens and pro-
motes the expectoration of the mucus and inflammatory
debris."

It has been so often demonstrated beyond the possi-
bility of a doubt, that the combined conditions making

up the climate of high altitudes do favorably modify the
causes and course of phthisis that the popular faith in
this "mountain cure" is almost unbounded by both the
lay and professional. El Paso offers many superior
advantages to the invalid and pleasure seeker, by reason of its well sheltered position from winds by its
mountain ranges and terraced hills on the north and
west, a slightly higher mean temperature and in a
notably less lower extreme range of this—absence of
the essential elements of volatized poisonous organic
matter and mechanically irritant particles, the uniformly
mild, dry air, which is bracing and exhilarating; so
many bright, clear, soft balmy days, never foggy, light
or little dews at night, rarely ice in winter, and more
rarely visited by snow. Equableness of temperature is
the rule; sudden changes are comparatively rare; well
provided with hotel and other accommodations, attractive
in itself, its mountain scenery, its singular mixture of
American push and Mexican indolence, mostly cosmopolitan, markets having an abundant supply of every
variety, with a quality of food all that can be desired.

Those ill-defined conditions included under the vague
title of delicacy of chest, may be completely removed by
residence in El Paso, as likewise the tendency to winter
attacks of bronchitis, chronic bronchitis in all varieties,
cirrhosis of the lungs, asthma, emphysema, hay fever
and chronic pneumonia, are always relieved, more often
cured, and the disposition to recurring attacks of
hæmoptysis effectually controlled.

Statistics afford us no guide yet to the rate and cause
of deaths among the native population, still it is a notable fact to a close observer, that pulmonary troubles
affect them to a very limited extent, the writer having
failed to find a case of consumption developed in this
climate after nearly five year's residence. The same is
true with regard to other diseases; that there are few

METEOROLOGICAL REPORT FOR EL PASO, TEXAS, FOR YEAR 1884.

	January	February	March	April	May	June	July	August	September	October	November	December	Annual Means
Mean actual barometer	26.380	26.253	26.197	26.183	26.204	26.220	26.237	26.288	26.239	26.305	26.345	26.216	26.253
Mean temperature	39.9	50.6	54.5	58.0	69.0	78.4	85.4	79.6	72.7	62.6	51.5	46.9	62.5
Greatest maximum temperat'e.	72.2	78.8	80.4	91.0	102.8	111.8	111.0	110.2	97.7	84.6	80.0	72.3	82.5
Lowest maximum temperature.	39.1	50.3	60.2	55.8	72.0	89.1	94.2	86.0	79.6	52.0	59.0	44.2	58.7
Average maximum temperat're	55.8	64.4	70.6	78.4	91.0	100.7	105.8	98.4	88.8	76.2	67.8	61.0	79.0
Greatest minimum temperat're	38.9	52.2	53.0	59.1	66.3	74.2	78.4	79.0	69.6	62.0	50.0	45.3	
Lowest minimum temperature.	11.8	22.2	26.4	35.9	39.5	57.4	66.4	63.3	49.0	37.1	25.4	27.4	
Average minimum temperature.	26.5	39.5	41.5	46.0	54.5	64.8	73.2	69.5	62.8	54.3	38.3	36.5	46.5
Mean relative humidity	58.7	47.3	36.8	31.9	26.7	34.4	85.6	48.0	55.2	71.1	60.0	51.9	3.8
Mean wind velocity	3.8	4.5	5.4	6.2	4.7	4.3	3.1	2.0	2.2	2.1	2.2	4.9	
Prevailing wind direction	W & NW	W	W	W	W	W	W	E	W	E	E	W	
Number of clear days	15	14	19	16	19	19	11	5	15	11	18	11	Total, 173
Number of fair days	13	12	9	13	10	9	16	16	10	12	10	13	" 143
Number of cloudy days	3	2	3	1	2	2	4	10	5	8	2	7	" 49
Rainfall (inches)	.55	.84	.23	.91	*	.11	.46	3.98	3.68	5.15	.22	2.07	18.3
Number of rainy days	6	6	8	5	5	10	10	17	11	15	3	10	
Max. rainfall in 24 hrs. (inches)	.36	.56	.19	.53	*	.10	.22	2.31	2.03	1.54	.18	.50	

* Rainfall inappreciable.

cases, most all of which recover, viz., typhoid fever, inflammatory rheumatism, sunstroke, hydrophobia, etc. Children's diseases are not so varied, and less severe than in lower altitudes. Diphtheria very rare; no case seen in El Paso in the last four (4) years; scarlatina rare and of a mild type, seldom, if ever fatal; never produces any of those ravages and after-effects so common in the East. The advantage of El Paso for pulmonary consumption in its incipient stages, and many other dreaded fatal diseases, has been too recently appreciated to allow extended statistics to be presented as to its benefits.

A meterological report for the year 1884, for El Paso, is herewith submitted (on opposite page) as an exhibit of the excellent climatic condition of this altitude.

FOOD.

As to food, the locality, together with the means of quick and preservative transportation, places at command everything, from the local abundant supply of fresh vegetables and fruits, including the delicious grapes of the country, with the grape wines equalling any in the world, to the northern products of the United States, and the numerous tropical productions of Mexico. The markets afford articles to meet every requirement of necessity or fancy.

ACCOMMODATIONS.

Accommodations as to home and family supplies, and rooms and board at the best managed hotels and private boarding houses, are commensurate with every demand made by the permanent resident or the transient sojourner. Rates are reasonable.

HOW LAND TITLES ORIGINATE—PRICE, ETC.

As already stated, Texas reserved by the treaty of annexation all her public domain, amounting to 171,967,-660 acres. Thus it was that while she was the youngest of States she was the most wealthy. From the earliest days of the republic it has ever been the policy of Texas to use her public lands for the encouragement of immigration, endowment of her school fund and the building of internal improvements in the State.

Each county has a local land office, with a surveyor, who is a bonded officer of the State. He keeps an accurate map of every survey ever made in his county, and a book in which every set of field notes is duly recorded, and patents (titles) to public lands come directly from the State. A portion of the county, perhaps one-third, belongs to the railroads, one-third to the State, and one-third to private owners, from all of whom good titles can be procured. Unimproved agricultural lands can be had, in any quantity, for from one dollar to five dollars per acre, according to location and advantages. Grazing lands from one to two dollars per acre. Lots in the city of El Paso from twenty-five to five hundred dollars for residences, and for business from ten dollars to one hundred dollars per front foot, according to advantages.

Titles are good. Nearly all controversies concerning titles have been settled by compromise or by the courts. Homesteads may be acquired wherever any vacant lands can be found, and each head of a family is entitled to 160 acres, by occupying and improving the same for three consecutive years. The laws of the State are similar to those of most of the advanced States of the Union. They give ample and full protection to life and property, and are rigidly enforced. The largest liberty of speech and thought is here encouraged and guaranteed; no proscription in religion or politics is tolerated; every right and privilege is closely guarded in the laws. All forms of religious worship may be practiced, and every shade of politics is entertained among our people. The two political parties are very equally represented by our population, and it is a question which has the ascendancy.

LAWS OF TEXAS OF GENERAL INTEREST TO IMMIGRANTS.

The homestead of a family, not to exceed 200 acres (not in any city or town), or town or city lot or lots, not to exceed $5,000 in value, exclusive of improvements at the time of their designation as a homestead, shall not be subject to forced sale for debts, except for taxes or for labor or material expended thereon. The owner, if a married man, cannot alienate the homestead without the consent of the wife.

PERSONAL PROPERTY EXEMPT.

All household and kitchen furniture; all improvements of husbandry; all tools and apparatus pertaining to any trade or profession, and all books belonging to public or private libraries; five milk cows and calves, two yokes of work oxen; two horses and one wagon; one carriage or buggy; one gun, twenty hogs, twenty head of sheep; all necessary provisions and forage on hand for the use of the family. And for every citizen not the head of a family, one horse, saddle and bridle; all wearing apparel, all tools, apparatus, and books belonging to his private library.

HOMESTEADS AND PRE-EMPTIONS.

Every head of a family who has not a homestead shall be entitled to 160 acres of land, as a homestead, out of any part of the public domain not included in any railroad reservation, or in any State section of land surveyed by virtue of any railroad land certificate, nor upon any island; upon condition that he or she select, locate and occupy the same for three years, and pay the office fees on the same. Any single man, twenty-one years of age, is entitled to 80 acres upon the same terms.

Any person who, in good faith, actually settles upon any part of the public domain, not exceeding 160 acres, and furnishes the Commissioner of the General Land Office satisfactory evidence that he or she has, in good faith, settled upon said land, shall be entitled to purchase the same from the State at one dollar per acre.

MARITAL RIGHTS.

All property, both real and personal, owned by husband and wife before marriage, remains the separate property of such owner, and such property as is acquired after marriage, by gift, devise or descent, becomes and remains the separate property to whom given, devised or descended. The homestead, or separate property, cannot be sold unless the wife joins in the conveyance.

All property acquired by either the husband or wife after marriage, except as above, is the common property of both. At the death of one party the survivor takes all, if there are no children; if children, the survivor takes one-half, the children the other.

SECRET SOCIETIES.

The city of El Paso is well represented in the secret
societies and organizations. The Masonic fraternity,
particularly, are in possession of one of the best fur-
nished halls in the Southwest, the entire third story of
the Mundy building.

Besides the following named societies, the founding of
Knights of Pythias, order of the "Eastern Star." Chosen
Friends, and a post of "G. A. R." is in contemplation.

For the benefit of members of those organizations into
whose hands this pamphlet may fall, we will give the
names of the presiding officers and secretaries of the
lodges here, so that they may correspond or communicate
with them should they desire to do so.

EL PASO LODGE OF PERFECTION, No. 5, A∴ A∴ S∴
R∴—S. W. Boring, 32° V. M.; Henry Berliner, 32°
Secretary.

EL PASO CHAPTER ROSE CROIX, No. 4, A∴ A∴ S∴ R∴
—Charles B. Patrick, 32° W. M.; Henry Berliner, 32°
Sec'y.

EL PASO COMMANDERY KNIGHTS TEMPLAR, No. 18.
—Charles Davis, Eminent Commander; T. L. Ennis,
Recorder.

EL PASO CHAPTER ROYAL ARCH MASONS, No. 157.—S.
W. Boring,·M. E. H. P.; Henry Berliner, Secretary

EL PASO LODGE, No. 130, A. F. AND A. M.—R. C.
Lightbody, W. M.; H. L. Bingham, Secretary.

5

El Paso Lodge, No. 284, I. O. O. F.—C. E. Fruin, N. G.; H. L. Capell, Recording Secretary.

El Paso Lodge, No. 2884, Knights of Honor.—Chas. F. Slack, Director; A. Kaplan, Recorder.

Rio Grande Lodge Knights and Ladies of Honor, No. 916.—Charles C. Kiefer, Protector; John S. Kierski, Secretary.

Order Railroad Conductors.—D. F. Rimmer, C. C.; F. A. Taylor, S. and T.

New Year Lodge, No. 135, B. of L. F.—C. McArthur. Secretary.

Besides the above societies, the founding of a Knights of Pythias Lodge, Order of the Eastern Star, Chosen Friends, and a Post of G. A. R. is contemplated.

ASSESSED VALUATION EL PASO COUNTY,
YEAR 1884.

Real estate improvements, city of El Paso—

Mills' map	$1,255,889	
Morehead's addition	78,345	
Satterthwaite's addition	65,600	
Magoffin's addition	89,820	
Campbell's addition	627,897	
Cotton's addition	40,400	
Bassett's addition	10,400	
Alexander's	6,175	
Hart's	61,050	
		$2,235,576
County real estate and improvements outside of city		1,378,329
Total real estate		$3,613,905
Railroads		1,888,481
Telegraph		15,900

Personal property in city and county—

33 jacks and jennies	342	
336 hogs	1,448	
1,379 horses and mules	42,405	
8,574 cattle	142,784	
3,200 sheep	8,029	
1,588 goats	2,291	
347 carriages and wagons	32,339	
Machinery, tools, implements, etc	76,100	
Goods, wares, and merchandise	481,000	
Money on hand	33,650	
Credits	63,228	
Miscellaneous	236,888	
		1,120,514
Total valuation		$6,638,800

AVERAGE TEMPERATURE, Etc.

	Average Temperature	Rainfall.	No. of Cloudy Days.
January, 1884	39.9	.55	3
February, "	50.6	.84	2
March, "	54.5	.33	3
April, "	59.0	.91	1
May, "	69.0	*	2
June, "	78.4	.11	2
July, "	85.5	.46	4
August, "	79.6	3.08	10
September, "	72.7	3.98	5
October, "	62.6	5.15	8
November, "	51.5	.22	2
December, "	46.9	2.07	7
January, 1885	41.7	.12	2
February, "	49.9	.03	1
March, "	56.6	.34	6
April, "	63.6	.04	4

* Too small to measure.

The following is taken from the report of the Chief Signal Officer of the Army for the 12 months ending June 30, 1883 :

El Paso, total No. of cloudy days for 12 months (year 1882)......... 30
Denver, Colo., "   "   "   " "   "   "   " 33
El Paso, total No. of cloudy days for 6 months ending June 30, 1883... 17
Denver, Colo., "   "   "   " "   "   "   " " " ... 36

IMPORTATIONS

MADE THROUGH THE EL PASO CUSTOM HOUSE FROM
JANUARY 1, 1881, TO DECEMBER 31, 1884.

DATE.	Free Goods.	Annual Increase.	Dutiable Goods.	Annual Increase.
1881	$3,920	....	$83,666	....
1882	10,626	$6,706	185,098	$101,432
1883	638,045	627,419	250,485	65,387
1884	821,394	183,349	374,522	124,037
Totals.......	1,473,985	....	893,771	....

RECAPITULATION :

Total free goods....... .... $1,473,985

Total dutiable goods   893,771

    Total importations, all classes $2,367,756

TABLE OF DISTANCES

From El Paso, Tex., to

	Miles		Miles
Abilene, Tex	455	Lerdo, Mex	515
Albuquerque, N. M	255	Lordsburgh. N. Mex	148
Aguas Calientes, Mex	860	Los Angeles, Cal	804
Atlanta, Ga	1,598	Marshall, Tex	795
Austin, Tex	879	Mexico City	1,224
Baton Rouge, La	1,074	Montezuma, Mex	112
Benson, Arizona	262	New Orleans	1,163
Big Springs, Tex	347	New York	2,410
Calera, Mex	767	Pueblo, Col	666
Camp Rice, Tex	53	Queretaro, Mex	1,071
Celaya, Mex	1,042	Raton, N. Mex	498
Chicago	1,639	Rincon, N. Mex	77
Chihuahua, Mex	225	San Antonio, Tex	632
Colorado, Tex	386	San Elizario, Tex	21
Colorado Springs, Col	711	San Francisco, Cal	1,286
Colton, Cal	746	San Juan del Rio, Mex	1,105
Dallas, Tex	648	San Marcial, N. Mex	152
Deming, N. Mex	88	Shreveport, La	835
Denver, Col	786	Sierra Blanca, Tex	92
Emporia, Kan	1,045	Silao, Mex	986
Fort Worth, Tex	616	St. Louis, Mo	1,359
Galveston	963	Topeka, Kan	1,107
Hot Springs, Ark	997	Toyah, Tex	194
Houston, Tex	848	Trinidad, Col	521
Jimulco, Mex	562	Tucson, Arizona	308
Kansas City, Mo	1,173	Washington, D. C	2,239
La Junta, Colo	602	Ysleta, Tex	12
Lamy, N. Mex	322	Yuma, Arizona	555
Las Cruces, N. Mex	44	Zacatecas, Mex	785
Las Vegas, N. Mex	387	Zeminez, Mex	371
Leon, Mex	965		

CLASS OF IMMIGRANTS WANTED.

We want population from every State in the Union, and from every country in Europe. We want the thrifty and industrious, with a few hundred or a few thousand dollars, to join us in occupying and building up the vacant places in our favored country, that they may secure pleasant homes for themselves and their families. We want them to identify themselves with our present population, and enjoy all the rights and privileges of the native born, which the laws of the State fully guarantee to them. We need population. We want immigrants of kindred races, that we may be a homogeneous people. We are all immigrants or their descendants. We give immigration credit for all we are or hope to become. We want especially persons skilled in farming, gardening and fruit growing. We want stock raisers, prospectors, miners, capitalists and manufacturers. We want capital to develop our unbounded resources, and take advantage of the many opportunities for profitable investment. We want immigrants who will bring along with them sufficient means and energy to enter upon business for themselves, to buy our cheap lands, become permanent residents, practical fruit growers and successful agriculturists, or who will follow some mechanical or manufacturing occupation. We want settlers who will rely on their own exertions and means. To such we say, Come; and if you have fair staying qualities your reward is sure.

FEMALE DOMESTICS

Are in great demand here, and we have no doubt that from fifty to one hundred good girls, or women, could at once obtain employment at wages ranging from fifteen to twenty-five dollars per month. This is entirely within bounds, and it is probable that a much larger number might obtain employment; and the demand will continue and increase from year to year. We would advise good domestics to come here. They will find this a most desirable place to cast their lot. The opportunities for good females of this class to make desirable settlements in life are excellent.

CONCLUSION.

In conclusion, we desire to say that it has here been our aim to give information concerning the geographical position and character of El Paso City and County, and the superior natural advantages which they possess, and which she offers with extended arms, open to receive and embrace in welcome all who may choose to cast their lot with ours.

First. For the peculiarly charming climate, free as it is from all and every epidemic; mild, yet invigorating, and singularly pure, pleasant and salubrious; where the yellow fever and cholera germs cannot exist; where sun-stroke is unknown; where a refreshing sleep can always be had; a perfect sanitarium, in fact, unsurpassed by any, probably, in the world.

Second. For her vast grazing domain, which is unsurpassed, as we have shown, by any on the continent.

Third. For her millions of tons of hidden treasure in the shape of gold, silver, lead, copper and coal, which lie buried within. the bosom of her majestic mountains.

Fourth. For her large bodies of agricultural lands. lying in one of the most fertile and beautiful valleys in the world, with so many attractions and advantages for the settler; with comparatively so few obstacles to overcome and hardships to endure, and with the many pleasant and easy conditions of life, so few dangers and privations incident to life on or near the frontier.

Fifth. For the commercial advantages possessed by the city, the great metropolis of this whole country, as has been shown, and to which we again invite attention.

We repeat, that no portion of our country offers greater inducements than this of which we have written, and of which far more might well be said. If we have failed to bring to light, or if we have misrepresented in any way, the advantages our situation offers, in the foregoing pages, it has been the fault of the head and not of the heart. And here we leave the subject, to be renewed at an early day, we trust, by a more able but not less impartial pen than ours.

THE MEXICAN CENTRAL RAILWAY

extends from El Paso, Texas, to the City of Mexico, traversing for over twelve hundred miles a vast elevated plateau or table land, rich with grazing and agricultural lands and abounding in mountains full of silver, iron, and other metals. The largest and most flourishing cities of the Republic are situated on the line of this great iron highway: Chihuahua, Santa Rosalia, Zeminez, Lerdo, Fresnillo, Zacatecas, Aguas Calientes, Lagos, Lerdo, Silao, Guanajuato, Irapuato, Celaya, Salamanca, Queretaro, San Juan del Rio, Tula, and the City of Mexico.

Durango, Guadalajara, San Luis Potosi, Saltillo, Pachuca, Morelia, and numerous other prominent cities are reached by stage and wagon, from points on the line of the Mexican Central. A great part of the territory traversed by this line enjoys the climate of the temperate zone. Extremes in temperature are almost unknown. A delightful coolness prevails in the shade. The nights are cool. Life and travel on the table land are equally agreeable, summer or winter.

MINERAL RESOURCES.

Famous, from the days of the conquest down to the present time, have been the mineral treasures hidden in the hills of Mexico. The dreams of adventurers are confirmed by the tests of modern science. Mexico is the richest country in the world in mineral resources. All the prominent metals have been found in large quantities, though as yet the search has been limited to the localities most easily accessible. A great deal of silver has been mined in Mexico, but there is good reason to believe that, notwithstanding Mexico has long been the great silver producing country of the world, the greater portion of her wealth remains undiscovered. It is undoubtedly true, also, that the country cannot long remain unexplored. The gates have been unlocked and thrown wide open. The average Western American is the undaunted explorer of modern times. There is, since the completion of the Mexican Central Railway and the introduction of modern mining machinery, no obstacle to his investigations in Mexico. The known existence of the precious metals in all the nooks and corners of a land of mountains, encourages a thorough investigation of the fastnesses and byways of the Republic.

Mexico's production of the precious metals is a subject which would require a volume, and can be only touched upon here. The mineral districts most distinguished for the production of silver and gold are those of Guanajuato, Zacatecas, Fresnillo, Chihuahua, and Durango, all reached via the Mexican Central. The districts of Guanajuato and Zacatecas form two groups, important for their numerous and industrious population. These districts, together with Chihuahua and Durango, abound not only in the precious metals, but in copper, iron, lead, zinc and tin.

Near the city of Durango is the Cerro de Mercado, a mountain 3,600 feet long by 1,100 feet wide—an area of 90 acres—and 640 feet high, containing the most remarkable deposit of iron in the world. It contains nearly 200,000,000 tons of iron ore, of remarkable purity.

There are large deposits of iron ore near Leon, and at the iron works near by some of the largest and finest ornamental castings in the world have been produced.

Mexico's mineral wealth undoubtedly lies in her vast

deposits of silver. Native silver has been found in considerable masses, sometimes weighing more than 200 kilograms, in the mines of Batopilos. It is frequently found in certain districts of Chihuahua, Guanajuato, and Zacatecas.

PRINCIPAL SILVER DISTRICTS.

Chihuahua: Batopilas, Batuchique, Candamena, Cusihuiriachic, Guadalupe y Calvo, Guadalupe de los Reyes, Jesus Maria, Morelos, Parral, Santa Eulalia, Toquimbo, Urique, Uruachi, Valle, Zapori.

Durango: Arzati, Avino, Bajada, Basis, Canelas, Coneto, Comercio, Cuencame, Durangal, Duraznito, El Oro, Fresnos, Gavilanes, Guanacevi, Huahuapan, Inde, Mapimi, Metatitos, Mezquital, Parrilla, Penon Blanco, Picoeterco, Pueblo Nuevo, Rodeo, San Dimas, San Juan de Guadalupe, San Lucas, Santiago, Sianori, Tamazula, Tejame, Topia, Ventanas.

Guanajuato: El Nayal, El Nopal, Gilmonene, Jesus Maria, La Joya, Mejiamora, Monte de San Nicolas, Rayas, San Pedro, Santa Lucia, Sirena, Socavon de San Cayetano, Valenciana.

Mexico: Chalchitepec, El Oro, Ixtlahuacan, Sultepec, Temascaltepec, Villa del Valle, Zacoalpan.

Queretaro: El Doctor.

San Louis Potosi: Bermalejo, Catorce, Charcas, Guadalcazar, Matehuale, San Pedro.

Zacatecas: Bolanos, Carcamo, Cedros, Chalchihuites, Fresnillo, Mazapil, Norio, Nieves, Sombrerete, San Juan de Guadalupe, Sierra Hermosa, Pinos, Rio Grande, Teul, Pico de Freire, Zacatecas.

The mineral districts given above are those from which was obtained the silver coined in the mints of the Republic.

SULPHURET OF SILVER

is found in Guanajuato, Pachuca, Zacatecas, and in Za-
culapan, State of Mexico. Ruby silver in Morelos, State
of Chihuahua. Black silver in Chihuahua, Guanajuato,
and Zacatecas. Argentiferous galenite in the greater
part of the mines of the Republic.

From the days of the ancient Aztecs down to the present time, gold has been found in nearly every part of
Mexico. It is found, both pure and mixed with silver
ore, and there is scarcely a single silver mine which does
not contain gold. Native gold is frequently found crys-
tallized in the silver ores of Villalpando and Rayas,
near Guanajuato; Guarisomay, west of Durango; and
Mezquitl, in Guadalajara.

Copper, lead, and sulphur exist in large quantities
along the line of the Mexican Central Railway, and
there are many indications of coal, though no good
workable bed has yet been discovered.

AGRICULTURAL PRODUCTS.

The mineral wealth of the Republic is so enormous,
and the pursuit of the precious metals is so alluring,
that the agricultural resources of Mexico are at present
less famous. Time will change this, as in the case of
California. Rich alluvial soils, natural fertilizers, nutritious grasses, abound; millions of acres yet untouched
Probably there is no country in the world, the natural
configuration of which is so advantageous for agriculture
as Mexico. It may be reasonably estimated that one-
half of the plateau upon which the Mexican Central is
built is valley or farming land. Where it is so, it is
very productive. Every tree, fruit, or plant of Europe
or North America will grow there. All domestic, or

other animals, whether imported or **native**, have **thriven
and multiplied.** Into the depressions and valleys the
tropical products intrude themselves, as oranges, bananas, limes, cotton, and cane. In the diversity of its
products, its wide extent, its extraordinary climate, its
freedom from diseases and climatic extremes, there is no
parallel, in any other region of the earth, to the great
plateau of Mexico.

If only one-fourteenth part of the territory of the
Republic were used for the raising of wheat and corn,
the annual yield would be about 110,000,000 bushels of
wheat and 400,000,000 bushels of corn every year; and
this immense yield would all be available for foreign
markets, as the outlaying lands have always raised
enough for home consumption. Besides, the Mexicans
are from choice a corn-eating people. Seven eighths of
the population live on tortillas.

Nevertheless, the tillage is all done with tools as ancient as Abraham — wooden sticks, the crotches of trees
shod with iron. Yet, an investigation of yield and quality make one wonder.

THE MAGUEY.

Beside these staple crops, a glance at some of the un-
common products of Mexico may not be uninteresting.
Nobody can have much of an opinion of the cactus
family as a thing of beauty or as a source of wealth.
In some parts of Mexico, the cacti assume gigantic
proportions and grotesque forms. One member of the
family is essential in daily life. The agave, aloe, maguey, or century plant, exists in some thirty varieties
and has more products than any other vegetable. It
produces in enormous quantities _pulque_, the national
beverage. 250,000 pints of this are consumed daily in
the city of Mexico alone. Each plant produces about

125 quarts of this juice, after which it dies. In other localities no juice or pulque is drawn from the plant, because its special virtues enable it to produce the brandy known as "Tequilla," from the locality on the Pacific Branch of the Mexican Central, where the best is produced. The mode of making this is as old as the Aztec civilization.

After the pulque has been extracted, the plant still posesses its greatest value. It can be made to yield an excellent quality of molasses superior to that yielded by the sugar cane. Still, the most valuable product is the fiber yielded by the leaves, equal to the best Yucatan jute. Where soil and locality do not admit of this use of the plant, it yet yields a pulp unequaled for making paper.

With only the maguey plant as a resource, Mexico might become one of the gratest cording, matting, and paper-making countries in the world.

THE RAMIE PLANT.

India is the original home of this plant, to which the climate and soil of Mexico are especially favorable, though it will grow wherever cotton will. Once planted, it is perennial for many years, and requires little cultivation or attention. It is not subject to destruction by worms and insects, and is cut four times a year. The fiber is stronger and finer than flax or cotton, and is considered for most purposes equal to silk. Each cutting yields as many pounds per acre as cotton does.

The India ramie, bleached, combed, and made ready for the spinners, brings in England about 50 cents per pound. This product must bear a prominent part in the commercial future of Mexico.

THE CASTOR BEAN

grows spontaneously and abundantly along the coast regions, though these are not the most favorable localities for its profitable cultivation. Every State of the Republic has land of the kind—an imitation of the temperate zone—in which it best thrives. The plant in Mexico yields the first year, and for about six months of the year, and the same plant lives and bears for about ten years, when it requires replanting. An acre of trees yields about 3,600 pounds of beans, or 1,800 pounds of oil.

TOBACCO.

It is not generally known that Mexico has been for many years a producer of tobacco of flavor which compares favorably with the best Havana. It must soon become an article of considerable value as an export, as, under the present condition of things, tobacco is produced in twenty-two of the twenty-eight States, and produces, as an export, more than $2,000,000 annually.

SUGAR.

The plant, once made, stands from ten to thirty years. It is under inefficient cultivation, but yields one-third to one-half more per acre than the island of Cuba. Nearly all the Mexican States produce it in greater or less quantity, and yet the present supply is inadequate to the enormous local consumption, and sugar brings a higher price than in the United States.

COFFEE.

In some localities the coffee plant demonstrates its adaptability to the climate by growing wild. Its best locality is about 3,500 feet above the sea, which indicates a wide range of territory. At that elevation it yields about three pounds to the plant.

Mr. Foster, late Minister to Mexico, stated in one of his reports that its quality was equal to the best known in any country, and that Mexico possessed in her coffee a far greater wealth than in her silver.

It is reliably stated that there are coffee plantations in Mexico that have annually borne for three-quarters of a century, without replanting.

In 1882 the amount paid by us for coffee was a little more than $46,000,000, of which nearly $30,000,000 went to Brazil.

COTTON.

This is one of the most ancient of the products of Mexico, and was raised, spun, woven, and dyed in brilliant colors by the Aztecs. Like all other products of this favored clime, the production bears no relation to the capacity of the country.

The Mexican Central traverses the Laguna country, one of the finest in the world for the growth of cotton. It now produces a large crop, and new areas are being planted every year.

The average yield per acre is about 15 per cent. more than in the United States. The cotton consumption is so prominent a factor in the calculations of the world's trade that it is useless to present again here familiar figures.

TROPICAL FRUITS.

These grow here in immense profusion and variety. Oranges, limes, and bananas are standard articles of consumption and trade, and the construction of railways renders their limitless supply from Mexico an important item. Several kinds of refrigerating cars are an undoubted success. The fruit trade from California (the same distance) in varieties which are mostly produced in all the States, is enormous. There is, in the near future, an immense development in the tropical fruit business of Mexico; fresher, cheaper, of greater variety and better quality, than we have ever been accustomed to. In the West Indies there is nearly a level surface of land. The crop per annum is a single one. In Mexico, one district has ripening fruit at one season of the year, and another district later or earlier. Around the city of Mexico, in addition to a list of tropical fruits whose names, variety, and deliciousness are a revelation to the stranger, strawberries, new potatoes, and green corn may be had every month of the year.

Of the dye-woods, medicinal products, hard and cabinet woods, cochineal, etc., produced naturally in Southern Mexico, it is useless to speak here. The terrible isolation of the country is finally broken. Already the country is awakening to a sense of the value and importance of products almost useless heretofore. Some time the agricultural wealth of Mexico, like that of California, will be found to far eclipse its riches in silver and gold.

The millions of acres of nutritious grasses, embracing a large part of Northern Mexico, part of the State of Chihuahua, and the Bolson de Mapimi, and extending northeast to the Rio Grande, are attracting the attention of American cattle-raisers, and already steps are being taken for the utilization of this vast grazing ground.

AS A RESORT FOR TOURISTS

AND HEALTH-SEEKERS,

Mexico offers great inducement. The tourist contemplating a European trip will do well to first note what Mexico offers.

Its beautiful cities, balmy climate, old churches and cathedrals, the peculiar and picturesque costumes of its people, its baths and healthful waters, all combine to make it most attractive to the tourist—more interesting than Spain or Palestine, Egypt or Switzerland.

As in Europe all roads lead to Rome, so in America all roads lead to El Paso, Texas, *the gateway to Mexico.*

RAILWAY RATES, Etc.

Full information regarding rates of fare, dates of excursions, and facts of every nature regarding this wonderful land, may be obtained upon application to

G. W. KEELER,
General Eastern Agent, 261 Broadway, N. Y.

A. C. MICHAELIS,
A. G. P. A., Mexico, Mex.

M. H. KING,
A. G. P. A., El Paso, Texas.

H. C. BARLOW,
Traffic Manager, Chicago, Ills.

E. W. JACKSON,
General Manager, Mexico, Mex.

ADDENDA.

EL PASO, TEXAS, Jan. 4, 1886.

Since writing the foregoing pages, the White Oaks Railroad project has so far matured that a corps of locating engineers will be put in the field within the next ten days, and the actual work of construction will follow within a month. It is the design of the great corporation who have undertaken this project, to push the work of construction as speedily as possible to a connection with the great Rock Island system, thus giving us another and an excellent route to St. Louis, Chicago, and all points north and east. This assures the future of El Paso and El Paso County, beyond all doubt or cavil. The hand-writing is on the wall; he who runs may now read. Pages might be filled with the attempt to enumerate all the advantages and benefits which we must derive from the completion of this great project, and we will only endeavor to mention a few of them, believing that the intelligent reader will understand how happily these things must affect us. It assures abundant and cheap coal for manufacturing and all purposes; cheap lumber, greatly increased railroad facilities and competitive transportation, and the development of a vast and rich country which, for hundreds of miles, must be tributary to El Paso. From these the sagacious men and the intelligent readers of all classes can read between the lines the innumerable benefits that must follow, and we will not now attempt to specify them.

We will also mention the fact that an enterprising colony of Californians have recently purchased a large tract of land in the valley about twenty-five miles below here, intending to commence the cultivation and canning of fruit on a large scale. This enterprise will no doubt be successful, as it is under the auspices of men of experience and ability.

The project for the construction of the great irrigating canal is also assuming shape, but the completion of the White Oaks Railroad will soon make this a necessity; the lands will be in demand, and the water must follow. In our next edition we hope to record favorable progress on these great projects.

(84)

www.ingramcontent.com/pod-product-compliance
Lightning Source LLC
Chambersburg PA
CBHW020315090426

42735CB00009B/1358